MY GREAT-GRANDFATHER DANCED BALLET

My Great-Grandfather Danced Ballet

Misha Solomon

BRICK BOOKS
PRINCE EDWARD COUNTY, ONTARIO

Library and Archives Canada Cataloguing in Publication

Title: My great-grandfather danced ballet / Misha Solomon.
Names: Solomon, Misha, author.
Identifiers: Canadiana (print) 20250285150 | Canadiana (ebook) 20250286432
| ISBN 9781771316675 (softcover) | ISBN 9781771316682 (EPUB)
| ISBN 9781771316699 (PDF)
Subjects: LCGFT: Poetry.
Classification: LCC PS8637.O4455 M92 2026 | DDC C811/.6—dc23

We gratefully acknowledge the Canada Council for the Arts, the Government of Canada through the Canada Book Fund, and the Ontario Arts Council and the Government of Ontario for their support of our publishing program.

ONTARIO ARTS COUNCIL
CONSEIL DES ARTS DE L'ONTARIO
an Ontario government agency
un organisme du gouvernement de l'Ontario

Ontario

Canada Council for the Arts
Conseil des Arts du Canada

Funded by the Government of Canada | Canada

Edited by Leah Horlick.
Author photo by Jean-Pierre Denault.
The book is set in Calluna, Calluna Sans, Didot, Benton Modern Display, Anisette STD.
Design by Kilby Smith-McGregor.

BRICK BOOKS
www.brickbooks.ca

CERTIFIED CANADIAN PUBLISHER

Though much of the work of Brick Books takes place on the ancestral lands of the Anishinaabeg, Haudenosaunee, Huron-Wendat, and Mississaugas of the Credit peoples, our editors, authors, and readers from many backgrounds are situated from coast to coast to coast in Canada on the traditional and unceded territories of over six hundred nations who have cared for Turtle Island from time immemorial. While living and working on these lands, we are committed to hearing and returning the rightful imaginative space to the poetries, songs, and stories that have been untold, under-told, wrongly told, and suppressed through colonization.

Table of Contents

OVERTURE 9

To my dear friend Rubin in Bucharest, 1937 30

Dog Star 33

Reading "Having a Coke with You" at My Best Friend's Wedding 35

Belongings 36

Yoo-Hoo 37

Sponsored Post; or, Grief 39

To my dear friend Ernest at sea, 1935 41

Mandrillus sphinx 43

A Failure of Science 44

Belongings II 45

Nineteen, Untouched 46

Dos and Don'ts of Dancing for the Modern Homosexual 47

To my colleague Ernest, for his eyes only,
in response to his confidential queries, 1934 49

The Seven-Year Itch 51

Shopping 53

A Recipe for Mug Cakes 55

Belongings III 57

Do You Know About the Flowers on the Corner
of Saint-Antoine and Berri? 58

Storytelling 60

Dear Mr. and Mrs. Banu, please give this to your son,
my new friend Rubin, 1933 62

Sienna 64

Belongings IV 66

The Limits of Fiction 67

ERNEST ♥ KR(~~ubin~~)YSTYNA; or, A Whole Life 75

To Riches 76

The Male Dancer 77

THIS ISN'T A GAY POEM. 79

Ernest Wonders 80

Postmodernity Is of Course a Euphemism for Internalized Homophobia 82

Our Man Rubin 84

Analytic Frameworks 86

Ernest Dances Siegfried in *Swan Lake* 88

(Help Me Choose a Photo of) My Engagement Ring (to Post on Instagram) 89

Heidi and Marcia and Mary and Cynthia 92

What Krystyna Knew 94

Julia Writes to Say 95

Yesterday Down at the Canal 96

THIS IS A POLITICAL POEM. 98

The House on Circle Road 99

Three Sonnets About the Art in My Home 100

History of the Jews in Quebec 103

The Seafood Buffet at Boca West Country Club, c. 1998–2010 105

Time Travel 107

I Try to Get My Grandfather to Tell Me Things His Parents Told Him 108

Our Father 110

Music 111

I'm a hole / I'm a pole / My great-grandmother was a Pole 112

THIS IS A CULTURALLY JEWISH POEM. 113

Meditations in an Emergency 116

The thing is I could save them but I don't 117

Notes and References 121

Acknowledgments 127

About the Author 129

(Rubin's Turn) 131

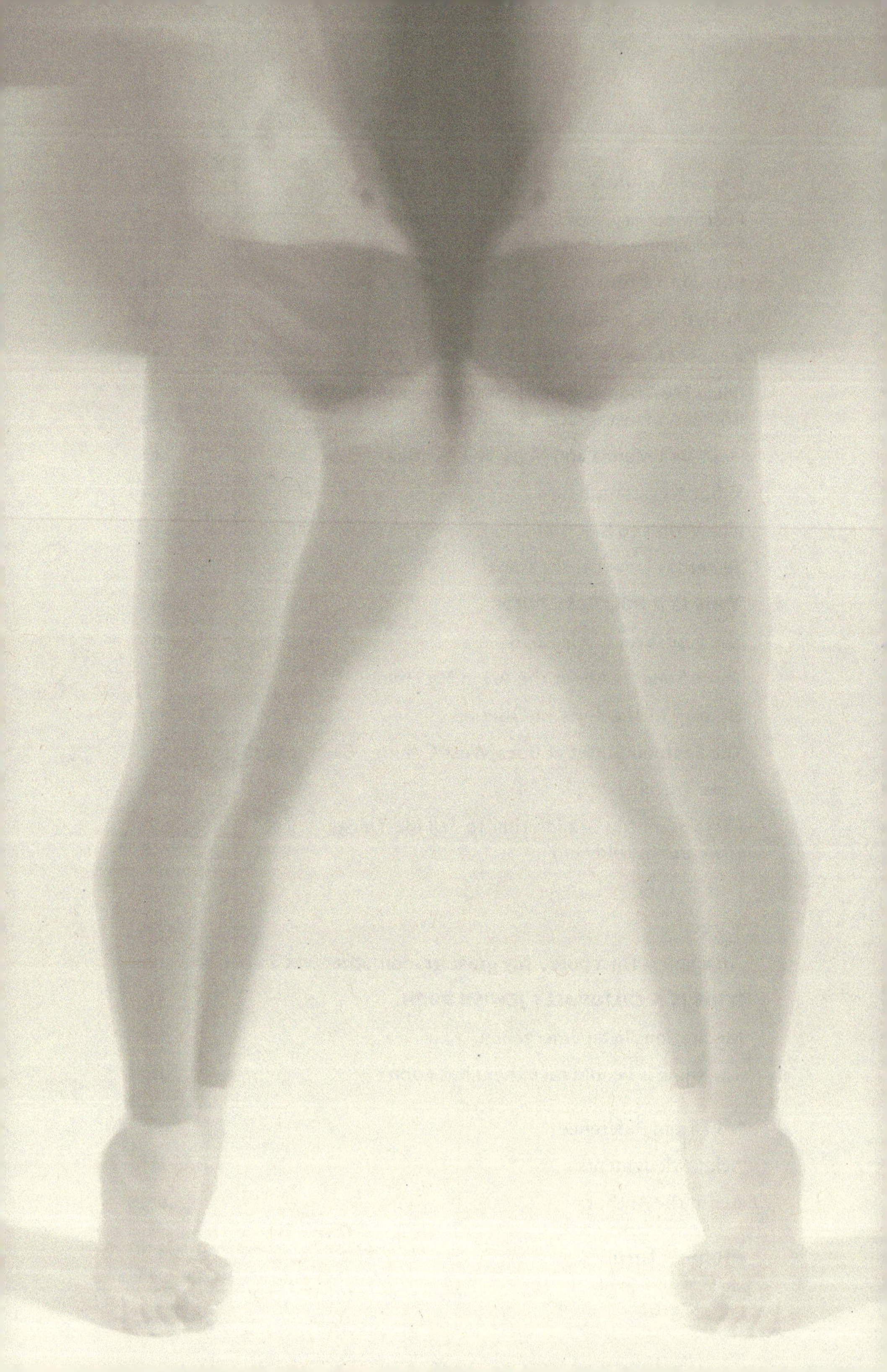

OVERTURE

When did you last feel like this?

a man a man a man a man a man a man
a man a man a man a man a man a man
a man a man a man a man a man a man
a man a man a man a man a man a man
a man a man a man a man a man a man
a man a man a man a man a man a man
a man a man a man a man a man a man
a man a man a man a man a man a man
a man a man a man a man a man a man
a man a man a man a man a man a man
a man a man a man a man a man a man
a man a man a man a man a man a man
a man a man a man a man a man a man
a man a man a man a man a man a man
a man a man a man a man a man a man
came here and they changed his name

When I was eight days old my parents paid a man to cut off a part of my penis while friends and family sipped tea and coffee from my then-already-dead-grandmother's good silver that my parents later sold in one of our downsizing moving sales and now I'm eight years deep in a relationship with a man to whom I explain that he can grip more firmly just below the head he's not going to hurt me I've already been degloved.

YES I WANT TO FEEL SAFE NO I DON'T WANT AN ETHNOSTATE YES OF COURSE I WANT AN EDEN

a a a a a a a the
man the man the
man the man the
man the man the
man the man the
man the man the
man the man the
man the man the
man the man the
man the man the
man the man the
man the man the
man the man the
man the man the
man the man the
man the man the
man the man the
man the man the
man the man the
man the man had
his name doubled

Dear Ernest,

Dear Rubin,

Dear Ernest,

Dear Rubin,

Dear Ernest,

Dear Rubin,

Dear Ernest,

Dear Rubin,

Dear Ernest,

Dear Rubin,

Dear Ernest,

Dear Rubin,

Dear Ernest,

I wet it with my own mouth.

I'm sorry I told you about my penis but I'm going to tell you more, OK? I wish I could have beautiful, elusive words, I wish I wrote something about the sea, I wish I could resist the urge to tell you that the man was my great-grandfather and his name became Herbert Herbert.

Most days, life is liveable.

How exciting to receive the Au Coq coupons when we had just been talking about rôtisserie chicken,

How exciting to buy a dog a condo a sweater a commissioned family portrait an insurance package a new wall-mounted AC unit a sweater a bouquet of fresh flowers a bouquet of fresh flowers a bouquet of fresh flowers,

How exciting to receive a generous rebate from Hydro-Québec for having purchased an energy-friendly AC unit,

How exciting to watch the flowers die knowing that means new flowers,

How exciting to still be able to say "tu m'excites tellement,"

How exciting to ignore the dog's barking during those last few thrusts,

How exciting to see a man in the park bend down to tie his shoe,

How easy it would be to ruin my life for that man, how easy comes that feeling of standing on a bridge and being sure you're going to jump even though you don't want to, how easy it would be and instead of dying I'd even get to cum,

I just want to dance in the ballet.

This is the only document the Canadian Jewish Archives could locate in reference to my great-grandfather.

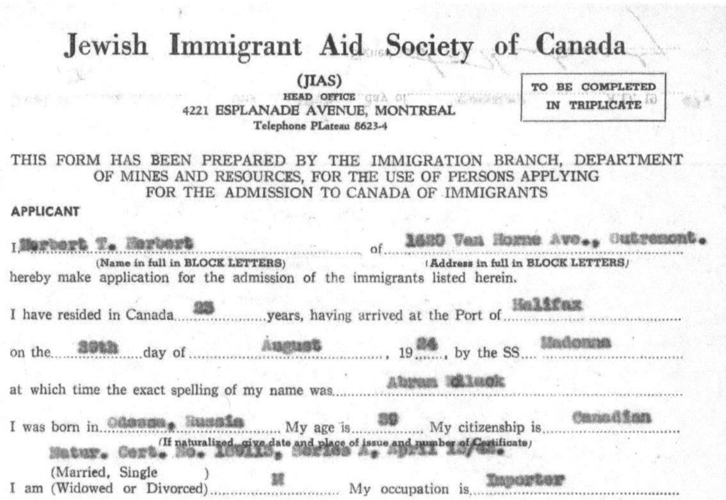

Jewish Immigrant Aid Society of Canada

(JIAS)
HEAD OFFICE
4221 ESPLANADE AVENUE, MONTREAL
Telephone PLateau 8623-4

TO BE COMPLETED IN TRIPLICATE

THIS FORM HAS BEEN PREPARED BY THE IMMIGRATION BRANCH, DEPARTMENT OF MINES AND RESOURCES, FOR THE USE OF PERSONS APPLYING FOR THE ADMISSION TO CANADA OF IMMIGRANTS

APPLICANT

I, Herbert T. Herbert of 1620 Van Horne Ave., Outremont.
(Name in full in BLOCK LETTERS) (Address in full in BLOCK LETTERS)
hereby make application for the admission of the immigrants listed herein.

I have resided in Canada 25 years, having arrived at the Port of Halifax

on the 29th day of August, 1924, by the SS Madonna

at which time the exact spelling of my name was Abram [illegible]

I was born in Odessa, Russia My age is 39 My citizenship is Canadian
(If naturalized, give date and place of issue and number of Certificate)
Natur. Cert. No. [illegible], Series A, April [illegible]

(Married, Single)
I am (Widowed or Divorced) M My occupation is Importer

Do you remember the *Phantom of the Opera* original cast recording? That white mask, that red rose? Of course you do, you were probably gay once too. The "Overture"—that's what this is, get it? I'm setting the scene. I used to listen on cassette. My mother took me to see the production in Toronto—her friend worked with a theatre producer who later went to prison for fraud and so we got great seats, right under where the chandelier swings climactically. I want you to be hearing a pipe organ. I want you to be waiting for a chandelier to fall.

Don't read this page. I told you, I wish I could be different.

~~Project Proposal~~

~~*My Great-Grandfather Danced Ballet* is a poetic exploration of queer longing, queer mundanity, and contemporary cultural Judaism. The project has two primary components: (1) epistolary, persona, and narrative poems that tell the story of Ernest and Rubin, two homosexual Jewish lovers in pre-Holocaust Romania, and of Ernest's later life in mid-twentieth-century Montreal; and (2) prose, lyric, and form poems that explore my homonormative existence in contemporary Montreal, including my relationship to my cultural Judaism, my romantic engagement(s), and my material comforts. These two components are connected by the fact that Ernest is a heavily fictionalized version of my actual maternal great-grandfather, Herbert, about whom I know very little save for the fact that he danced ballet in Romania before immigrating to Montreal. The two components intersect in metapoems that explore my queer longing: my desire to discover that my homosexuality, my queerness, is shared with a member of my family. The project is inspired by other contemporary texts, such as Casey Plett's *Little Fish* and Lisa Richter's *Nautilus and Bone*, that also seek to reposition familial or Jewish history in a queer context, and by media such as Bianca Stigter's documentary *Three Minutes: A Lengthening* and Sebastian Meise's drama *Große Freiheit (Great Freedom)*, both of which explore mid-twentieth-century Judaism and/or queerness using new and innovative lenses.~~

THIS IS A STORY
THAT IS TRUE

Speaking of, I've been listening to *The Phantom of the Opera* lately and the Phantom is definitely subtextually gay. Diva worship gone violent? Body shaming another man? A toxic queen if I've ever heard one.

See how easy this is? How much fun? How facile? How dangerous? Dangerous? Why dangerous? Is it *offensive* to be *accused* of being gay? I see how it is.

the man man man man man men were in love, are in love, I move them across a stage and their love seems so true I convince myself for a moment that I really do exist

Last week, my mother went to visit my great-aunt while she was recuperating from spinal surgery. My mother mentioned my project to her, and my great-aunt mentioned in kind that her father once flew a plane. Most of this project has already been written, however, and so that detail won't figure in here anywhere.

we'll
go this
afternoon,
which colour
would you like?grow
out your moustache.so did he
start this fight, or what?I know
I'm on the list.I don't get it either.

a nectarine

A DOG

my dog

my nectarine

LET'S SHAKE HANDS

let's die together

a seafood buffet

MY SEAFOOD BUFFET

a man

the man

Herbert Herbert

ERNEST ERNEST

the

men the

sea the

sea the

moon the

moon the

ocean the

ocean the

ship the

ship the

land the

land the

house the

house the

love the

love the

home the

home the

sea the

sea the

sea

the sea

the

To my dear friend Rubin in Bucharest, 1937

You will notice first the stamp,
I hope you keep it safe;
I had to pry it from my stockbook.
Krystyna would know three cents were missing
and she would be displeased.

As I have said in letters previous,
you would like Krystyna.
She is thrifty and Polish
and Jewish, despite her name.
My last name is different now

and you will laugh when I tell you
(I do so miss your laugh,
please tell me if you laugh)
that my name is Ernest Ernest.
So you can call me Ernie still

but Ernzweig was hard for the goyim,
and for me,
and my boss decided I should just double up.
You would not like my boss,
although he is Jewish—

but born here, in Montreal.
He does not think I am a very good salesman
and neither do I,
and neither does Krystyna,
and neither would you,

although I did manage to sell you
on my companionship, didn't I, Rubin?
I do so miss your companionship.
I sell table linens door-to-door
and I do not sell very many.

Do you remember
when we danced
the pas de deux from *Swan Lake*
after the others had left the studio?
Last week,

I danced it with a large tablecloth
and woke Krystyna from bed when I knocked
a candlestick from the table.
I told her I was trying to fold the schmatta
and she just shook her head.

But you would like her!
She dyes her hair a fiery red
and she has the best taste
in clothes. She wants to open up a dress shop
after we have children and they grow.

Rubin, come meet Krystyna.
You must try to leave, Rubin.
I hope the company is touring
and that is why you have not answered.
The papers do not talk much of Romania

but what they do say sounds frightful.
Come meet my wife, Rubin.
She would love to see you dance.
I have told her how much better
a dancer you are than I am.

I hope you have found a girl, Rubin.
I hope you come here
with your girl
and she and Krystyna could be such great friends
and you would sell so many more linens

than I do.
Come sell linens with me, Rubin.
There are mostly fine people here
and our children could be such great friends
and I worry

that my letters are not reaching you.
Save the stamp, please, Rubin.
I did not use a sponge,
though that would surely have been safer.
I wet it with my own mouth.

Dog Star

In French, a heatwave is a canicule,
same origin as our dog days,

something about Sirius,
the brightest star in the sky.

To talk about the star's rising
is talk of the cynic cycle,

to talk about a facial tic resembling
a snarl is talk of a cynic spasm,

to doubt the relevance of all this
to your own life is to be

cynical, in a sense. This was,
in a sense, the punchline, in

the sense a poem has a punchline, or
this poem has a punchline. Smoke

is a solid, in the same way, in a
sense, that a tomato is a

fruit. Knowledge is knowing
a tomato is a fruit; wisdom

is not trying to grab a handful
of smoke. A fun game for a gnat

would be to catch smoke in
a tiny net. When you were

a child did you catch butterflies?
Did you stare up at the stars?

Did you know your dreams would
float away, neither solid nor liquid

nor gas? Did you know your dreams
were for naught? Once, after drunkenly

buying fries at Pommes Frites in
the West Village, my friends and

I huddled under the balcony of
some older twentysomethings

who ashed their cigarettes on us.
As my friends protested, I yelled

up "have fun realizing your dreams
are for naught." This was the wisest

I have ever been. They probably
didn't hear me. And back then I hadn't

even read up on the Dog Star. When
you were a child, did you have dreams?

Reading "Having a Coke with You" at My Best Friend's Wedding

after Frank O'Hara

is even more fun than yada yada yada—
it was great, though
and Bill Somethingberg who lives in
my best friend's parents' building
thought I did a fantastic job and
he would know, he studied poetry
in undergrad at Columbia (I went there too, Bill)
where he's now the head of something medical

partly because Bill thought I wrote
the poem, partly because the wedding
was in one of the first Ashkenazi synagogues
in the US, partly because the synagogue
is actually a museum, partly because I absolutely
won the wedding talent show (ask Bill)

except possibly for the reminder that I don't
live in New York, I never really lived in New York
I dabbled in New York for four years, except possibly
most of the wedding attendees have been to San Sebastian
and/or Irún and/or Hendaye and/or Biarritz and/or Bayonne
and I never have and maybe never will, except possibly
I once thought I was in this world even though I knew I wasn't of
it but looking down from the bima it seems that I was cheated
of some marvelous experience I never knew I could have had
which is why I'm telling you about it

Belongings

He won't eat the spare ribs she's made and she tells him he's not American enough and because it's a warm evening and because business is good and because the children won't stop hugging his legs, instead of getting up from the table and mumbling something about the fact that they're not even living in America, he says "let's go to New York City" and it makes him sad, for a moment, how happy she looks, how long it's been since her eyes shone with something quite akin to joy, the moment's gone, Krystyna is happy and the house is happy and the travel agency is happy to book them on a weeklong trip to New York City and Margot wants to ride the Cyclone over and over and Izzy claps at every yellow taxicab he sees and one morning the kids are so exhausted from the riding and the clapping that they let Ernest read the *New York Times* the bellhop brought up to their room and on Page 7 Ernest reads the title "Rumania Summons Jews" and the lede "Labor Service Will Begin Monday," the day they'll return to Montreal, and Ernest calls Krystyna over "Krystyna, Krystyna, come see" and shows her the ad, just below, for a muskrat-lined coat with a wool tweed exterior, available in red, green, or brown, selling at Saks Fifth Avenue for just $195.00 and says "we'll go this afternoon, which colour would you like."

Yoo-Hoo

Yoo-hoo, do you love me?

Do you love me, yoo-hoo, do you love me, do you love what I'm wearing?

Yoo-hoo, you in the tank top, you in the tank top and the lavender hair, you sitting on the same café patio reading the novel I finished reading yesterday, do you want to talk about the novel?

Do you want, yoo-hoo, do you want to hear what I thought about the novel? Yoo-hoo, if you look my way maybe I'll say "yoo-hoo, I just read that novel, and I thought it was transformative/underwhelming/derivative/groundbreaking."

Yoo-hoo, do you see me, do you see me over here? I wore this tomato-red shirt so you could see me, yoo-hoo, you with the well-dressed baby, you look like you know nice shirts, yoo-hoo, do you want to tell me you like my shirt?

Over there, you over there, yoo-hoo, do you want to ask me what I'm working on? I just bought this new notebook to write one poem per day, but, yoo-hoo, I've only written the date and my name and now I'm staring thoughtfully past you hoping you'll think I'm actually staring at you and you could say "yoo-hoo, why are you staring at me" and I'd say "how embarrassing, yoo-hoo, I'm actually staring past you, thoughtfully, thinking thoughts, by the way, do you have the time, I didn't bring my phone, I'm trying to be more present?"

Yoo-hoo, do you have the time? Yoo-hoo, do you want to know why I need the time? I don't look like someone who needs to yoo-hoo for the time, isn't that intriguing?

Yoo-hoo, do you want to know?

Yoo-hoo, do you want?

I want, yoo-hoo, I want so much, yoo-hoo, you with the sexy calves, do you want me? Yoo-hoo, you can't have me, but I want a little yoo-hoo, I'd love a little yoo-hoo.

Sponsored Post; or, Grief

Guillaume brings me one (1) Quaker Crispy Minis White Cheddar Flavour Large Brown Rice Cake on an IKEA DINERA light pink side plate (8").

"Thank you, merci, Guillaume, my fiancé" I say.

Earlier, my fiancé Guillaume and I were working on a one-thousand (1000)-piece jigsaw puzzle by Fits (stylized as *fits*, in cursive font). All of Fits' "small-batch puzzles" "feature unique art from artists around the world." This puzzle, the one the love of my life Guillaume and I have halfway completed, is called Tiger Queen and the "illustration was done by Lay Hoon Ho from Vancouver, Canada."

The puzzle comes in a light pink box. It is the same shade of pink, often called Millennial pink, as the IKEA DINERA side plate (8") off which I ate my one (1) Quaker Crispy Minis White Cheddar Flavour Large Brown Rice Cake. It is the same shade of pink as the upper layer of the HAY Pillar Candle (designed by Lex Pott) that my amazing partner Guillaume bought me for my thirtieth (30th) birthday.

My uncut lover Guillaume and I are raising our lack (0) of children in an interfaith (2) household and so earlier we attempted to dislodge the hardened wax from the candle cups (9) of our Via Maris Trace Chanukiah (currently out of stock) in a colour they call clay, which is in fact a crepuscular shade of Millennial pink. We also have an indoor non-denominational wreath, which was expensive, but not at all pink.

I am so lucky to have such a devoted same-gender life partner and to be surrounded by the colour that has come to define my very generation. For instance, my IKEA DINERA side plate (8") is not alone—it came alongside six (6) plates (10"), five (5) other side plates (8"), and six (6) bowls (6") (large enough for a dinner portion for my lithe and increasingly toned fiancé Guillaume but a bit small for me). When I showed my best friend Lexa, with whom I attended Columbia University in the City of New York, and alongside whom I graduated summa cum laude, a photo of the puzzle, she said "of course you have a trendy puzzle that matches your home decor." I am so lucky to have such friends and such a reputation!

Still, I often wonder about my foreskin. It, too, would have been Millennial pink, and I believe, had it not been taken from me, that my life may have been even more complete.

To my dear friend Ernest at sea, 1935

Mazel Tov! You made it aboard
without losing your trunk. I
would owe Otto five lei if you
were to respond to this letter.
Ernest, do not respond.

Only Otto believed in you; I and
everyone else at the company
were sure you'd leave your
trunk at home or set it down and
forget where you put it. I always

told you Otto held you in high
esteem. It's not about the money,
I just think it would be best
for you to start anew. You might
hate me right now, I was unkind

last week. But what would coming
with you have accomplished? Across
the ocean they might not be killing
Yids but there's nowhere to my
knowledge where they are kind

to me. You are imagining grabbing
my hands and saying "to us, Rubin,
to us" but we both know that you
can wear us like a shawl, take us
off when you feel too warm, but I am

me no matter how sweltering it is.
The girls in Canada will love you,
Ernest, you'll find some gorgeous
shiksa and raise a blue-eyed son
who'd sooner wring my neck

than shake my hand. I am being
unkind again, Ernest. This letter
was to be tender but tenderness
would not be true, would it?
Tenderness takes time and we

never had much of that. Show
your wife tenderness. All I ask
is that you show your wife
tenderness and that just once
you think of me. In the privacy

of your marital bed, when you
have finally gotten your baby
to sleep and you have hours
to do nothing but be tender
think of me. But don't think

of me in the storage closet
of the studio. Don't think
of me on my knees in a
farmer's field. Think of me
there with you then. You are

imagining grabbing my hands
and saying "but you could
be there with me, Rubin" but
I will not respond to that as my
response would be unkind.

I ask so little of you, Ernest.
I ask only that you think
me into tenderness and that
you never respond to this letter.
Grow out your moustache.

Mandrillus sphinx

A mandrill has a beautiful face,
the red, the blue—that mask
a sexually selected rendering
of toxic masculinity, that pretty
face would rend you limb from
limb.

A mandrill's tender scrotum
is neon lilac and when they bend
over their ass is a rainbow and
the males tend to be twice
the size of the females.

Sometimes I feel gender's tendrils
overtaking me, I grow a lush moustache,
a benediction of maleness, I wish
my masculinity came with more colours,
I wish sometimes to be a bender, to
wear nail polish and dresses like the
jocks do now, the biggest mandrills
embracing their effete balls,
but I'm small and I
can't control my diction.

A Failure of Science

My little dog once was smaller,
lived inside his Shih Tzu mother,
was born and grew and now
kicks grass after he urinates,
a reflex from deep within.

It took centuries, millennia
to make my little dog,
his mother made to sit on royal laps,
his Yorkie father made to rat,
bred and inbred and crossbred to make
a dog made for nothing at all.

Made for me and my fiancé,
if you believe in something like fate,
two men who can't make anything
when we make love.

My little dog's mother made milk for him—
I'd have let his needle teeth
tear up my nipples.
All I want is to make
things, not with my hands
but with my body.

Belongings II

Ernest's boss just waves him off when Ernest tells him he has to take a long lunch to go to a meeting at his son's school, he has to rush to pick up Krystyna even though he told her he could just leave her cash for a cab, but she doesn't like the way the drivers look at her, they make it to school and Ernest pauses suddenly before grasping the door handle, feels like the metal handle will burn his hand, when they get to the principal's office he feels sick to his stomach, the stern gentile in his goyishe tweed barely looks up at them, Ernest prides himself on knowing when he isn't wanted—he had left his home, hadn't he, had left Rubin well enough alone, mostly, since the letter—and he feels mostly wanted in his adopted home, save for some rolled eyes, at first, from certain more established Jews when he couldn't think of a word and reverted to Yiddish, save for, sure, the occasional "fuckin' Yid" and hard shove from an astute Irishman when he had to venture to their neighbourhoods, but for the most part the landed Jews helped and clothed and fed him, the Québécois were charmed by him, especially the women, and sometimes the men, and most importantly they all made their wanting or not abundantly clear, but now, at the Protestant school his children, honorary Protestants in the eyes of the school board, had no choice but to attend, the school that had asked him and Krystyna to both come in, for him to take off work, to talk about the fighting Izzy was doing, he's forced to stay somewhere his body, or maybe the place itself, is telling him to flee, the principal says, as cheerily as he can, that he's used to their way of child-rearing, says "well we don't think of behaviour in those terms" when Krystyna, frustrated by the lengthy description of her child's interactions with other children, asks sharply "so did he start this fight, or what?"

Nineteen, Untouched

You're too smart to be a virgin, but that's just another story,
an easy fix, dorm walls are thin and would a virgin
ask the hottest guy on the thirteenth floor to cum on his face
and afterwards meet up with friends at the Seinfeld diner
and stage-whisper that he needed to wash his hands
because they smelled like ass?

Your favourite security guard is working
at the entrance to your dorm, and you want
to tell her that there's dried semen on your neck,
but really you want to tell her
that you've finally been touched,
but really you want to tell your mother
that you've finally been touched,
but your mother is asleep
in a different country and in eighth grade,
when you knew all the answers in sex ed,
the other boys thought it was cooler
that you learned everything from porn,
not caring, open conversation.

At nineteen, you thought it had gotten to be too late
so you traded in your innocence
and really you were twenty, but even now,
you're telling stories.

Here's a story it's far too late to tell:
two boys take each other gently by the hand.
One of them looks just like you.

Dos and Don'ts of Dancing for the Modern Homosexual

Do participate in the horah. It's so easy, and you've been doing it since before your own bar mitzvah. It's the perfect dance to fade into the background, or to take your rightful place as court jester. Clap the loudest! Kick your legs the highest! All is fair game in the horah. And when it comes time to lift the child-adult or wedded couple into the air, you can grab a chair leg and show how masculine you still are, or retreat to your gaggle of gal pals, giggling and ogling.

Don't listen to your friend when she tells you to just go up to any guy and start grinding with him, even if it's your first time at a gay club and she has so many gay friends. Consent matters, even on a dance floor redolent of semen and amyl nitrate, and you'll be forever haunted by the confused and dismissive look that otter gives you.

Do queen it up at straight events you attend as a platonic date for a female friend, including but not limited to the Kappa Alpha Theta sorority formal (twice), a Slovenian ball in Montreal, the Trafalgar School for Girls prom (one year before your own prom, four years before you come out). Be the faggot they want you to be, you owe them that. They like when you do a little body roll, when you Jersey Turnpike up against your date.

Don't stop dancing at these aforementioned events until your date is good and drunk and that one gay swimmer from Sig Nu catches your eye.

Do or **Don't** take it as a compliment when your friend's boyfriend tells you, at a wedding in your thirties, that you dance as if you were straight.

Do or **Don't** reply that you just can't drink like you used to, and so you're not drunk enough to dance faggily.

Do let the music move you when "Don't Stop Believin'" comes on. Lock eyes with Lauren and know you're both remembering that New Orleans trip, mime every lyric. Remember your youth while you're still young, remember the premiere of *Glee*, the advanced preview in May 2009 that you watched with your mother, the possibilities it seemed to allow for even though you weren't in high school anymore, the promise it seemed to have before it became problematic in retrospect.

Don't stop believin'; hold on to that feelin'. Streetlights, people.

Don't stop believin'—hold on. Streetlights, people.

Don't stop believin'. Hold on to that feelin': streetlights, people.

Do slow dance with your fiancé. It will be a little awkward, since you don't really know who should lead, or how to hold each other, or how to slow dance, really. Slow dancing was never for you, and slow dances are hard to come by after prom. You're not used to public displays of affection like this.

Don't separate your bodies just yet. Hold on to that feeling. Also, you have an erection. Hold on.

To my colleague Ernest, for his eyes only, in response to his confidential queries, 1934

Your reading of this letter is predicated upon your having
safely arrived home, which is predicated upon the țuică
not having completely overwhelmed your ability to walk.
The țuică also filled you with questions, which rendered me
uncharacteristically speechless. I'd like to blame the țuică, but

I was having such fun watching you imbibe that I simply
forgot to drink. No, it seems you've found a way
to shut me up, without having to stuff anything
in my mouth. You asked, and when you asked your eyes shone
and I saw in them the earnestness—ha!—

the Ernestness of a younger you. You asked why I liked
you, or in fact you asked why I was wasting my time with
you, and when I rolled my eyes, you rephrased, but the reason
I didn't answer isn't because I don't know the reasons. I know
the reasons. I like you with all of my senses.

I like the way you look, your skin shaded brown
with the persistence of your pilosity. I like the way
you look looking at me, your being brimming with a hunger
so different from the fanged appetite I've seen in other men,
more like the hunger of an old, old dog, if you'll forgive me,

who has lost all his teeth, yet cannot wait to gum
his meagre meal. Moving down the face, I like the way
you smell, onions just beginning to sweat
in hot butter, the gentle liquorice of dill, and once
your clothes are off, the forest moss after a rain.

I like the way you taste, your salty neck,
your briny cock, you're blushing now, if you
weren't already, the sweetened dairy of each
toe. I'm a gentleman, so I'll speak not
of your jism. I like the way you sound,

especially when your lips are very close
to my ear and I hear so much in the silence
of your breath. I like the way you feel, like corn starch
mixed with water, solid between my fingers
but threatening to come apart.

The reason for my silence lies in the secret
encoding of this letter. It's a very simple code in fact:
simply replace each use of "like" with "love,"
including in the following phrase: I like you far too much
for any time we spend together to be anything near waste.

This would be a lovely place to end the letter, but
I feel compelled to answer your other query. Yes,
I have been with gentile men. I know you well enough to know
there's some reason that you asked, but I don't yet know
you well enough to know what that reason is. So all I'll say

is that there's something about their foreskin
that makes them seem more masculine, at first, but
then leaves you with the feeling that it's quite coquettish
how they hide themselves behind a sheath of skin, like a schoolgirl
giggling behind her hand after sending a note to a boy she likes.

The Seven-Year Itch

You should know, my love, that when I jerk off to r/faceandcock on the toilet at midnight, there are no faces within I'd rather kiss than yours.

No one told me getting everything
I ever wanted would never be enough. No one
told me that once I got a boyfriend

I'd have to be in a relationship.
What's the fag translation of Borat's "mah wife"?
How can we queer "to the moon, Alice"?

This is my life: I run my tongue
along the same stranger's skin until I taste
something like understanding. I love you,
I love you, I love you, but sometimes,
in the middle of the night, I wish I didn't
know your name.

You should know, my love, that I've always been faithful; I haven't even flirted, and not just because growing up in the age of internet dating means that I don't know how to.

I'm almost as old as you were when we met,
when you told me you couldn't tell me that we'd be together
in a week, a month, a year. I'm almost as old as my father
was when I was born.

But that's neither here nor there, is it? Is it
funny when I respond "we just keep trying!"
to the question of if and when?

Is it funny that oftentimes I would like another
being in the home, but that sometimes I want
it to be a baby we'd raise and sometimes I want
it to be an adult you'd watch me fuck?

*You should know, my love, that I love you more and more each day, but that
I like you depending on the moon, how much you complain about work,
whether you let me near you when you're unwashed.*

Let's keep doing this: I'll cook and you'll clean
and we'll only fight about the dog. You'll take
too long to match your socks to your shirt and I'll give
you a hard time for not understanding when I do
and don't like coconut.

We've never shaken hands, isn't that odd?
Maybe that's the problem, let's start
again. It's nice to meet you, would you like to die together?

Shopping

We buy a speckled ceramic vase for his mother
and then we buy a new vase for ourselves.

The vase we buy ourselves is glass, hand-blown,
twisted and prismatic. There's an Italian word for it, surely.

Before this glass vase we had a ceramic vase:
floral and Millennial pink, yet vaguely 70s.

We grew out of it. And before that now-tacky vase
we didn't have a shared vase.

I had a simple glass cylinder in my old studio. Someone
else was done with it, and I never used it.

Before I took that vase from the giveaway pile
in my old job's kitchen, dinosaurs roamed the Earth.

There were those that walked, like the stegosaurus,
with those leafy spikes, and those that flew,

like the pterodactyl, who was just hoping to be home
in time for dinner, and those who swam,

like Jeannine. And then the dinosaurs were gone,
and some little shrew got smart, and climbed a tree,

and came back down, and stood straight up, and blamed
his wife for his new problems. And then to apologize,

he brought her flowers, a gorgeous assortment, a fiery bouquet
of roses and marigolds and goldenrods and then,

for many years, I was alone with my free vase,
and then we loved a pink vase, and now

we're not quite sure which flowers would look best.

A Recipe for Mug Cakes

Making a mug cake is very simple.
All you need is one banana, one egg, two
tablespoons of cocoa powder. All you
need to do is unpeel the banana and
put it in a mug and mash it with
a fork and crack the egg into the mash
and measure two tablespoons of cocoa
powder and mix it all together and microwave
it for ninety seconds. Making a mug cake
is very easy but sometimes the banana is
frozen so you need to let it defrost on the
counter first and then the unpeeling hurts
your fingers because the banana is still
quite cold and often you spill cocoa
powder all over the counter and cocoa
powder is always tricky to clean up and
you could leave it for your fiancé to
do but you said you'd make these
mug cakes for the two of you even though
there's a perfectly tasty real cake sitting
in the freezer waiting to be eaten and
you're worried if you don't eat it soon it
will be freezer-burned but he says that's
not a thing that happens to desserts, that
your parents made that up and also the
cake is full of sugar and butter but the mug
cake has no added sugar and no butter at
all and butter is your favourite food but is a
source of deep stress for your fiancé so
you make these chocolate-banana omelettes
in two souvenir mugs (one professional, one
academic) and you add some rainbow sprinkles
to make it clear these are desserts and not

punishments and you eat the mug cakes hot
hot hot, as hot as the banana was cold, and
now your fingers and the roof of your mouth
are both numb. Your dog is also named
Mugcake, did I mention that? Because
you love mug cakes so much. Mugcake
is peeing on the floor. Mugcake is trying
to lick the inside of your nose. Mugcake is
lying between the two of you on the couch
and you're both petting his belly and you
look up and kiss a mug cake crumb off
the corner of your fiancé's smile.

Belongings III

I was supposed to be the mayor at minimum and now my daily achievement is holding off on jerking off until I can write an erotic poem about my great-grandfather, or some made-up version of him, writing this poem instead of that one, even, because googling "1940s name for male sex worker" felt a little too close to "old-fashioned word for semen," the search that was on my screen when Guillaume walked into our home office the other day, an hour or so after I had stormed into the office from the dining room because the sound of him eating a grapefruit section by section was distracting me from the important writing I needed to be doing, because googling "1940s name for male sex worker" brought up too many questions about positionality—I've never hired a sex worker or done sex work, who am I to write about it, but is thinking I need to be implicated in sex work to write about sex work othering sex work, I'd write about being a dentist, for instance, but dentists aren't marginalized, but they are diminished in some way, they make good money but high rates of suicide, right, that's a thing, and maybe tacit antisemitism too—and this is what I've come to, writing my little poems, always telling, struggling to show, plot as pathos, this is all for me but I want you to love it, I need you to love it, it's accessible, right?, even if you don't like poetry you're enjoying this and if you do like poetry you're appreciating the way I'm, I don't know, shaking the poetry tree and letting the crabapples fall all over me, some overripe and squelching to the ground, some bruising, some drawing blood, and the blood is pooling around me now, you're lapping at it, I hope, I can't see straight because of the fruit-related concussion and the blood loss, I was supposed to be the mayor, did I say that already, my mother's seamstress coworker-slash-friend Sylvie Lauzon always said that, called me "le maire de Montréal" when I was eleven, Sylvie had all gay friends, even her ex-boyfriend she still lived with was gay, and maybe those gays should have taken me aside, whispered "we know what you are, you're one of us, we'll show you our ways," maybe if they had I wouldn't be fading fast on this forest floor, wondering if my not-great-grandfather was a top or a bottom or vers.

Do You Know About the Flowers on the Corner of Saint-Antoine and Berri?

You know, on the corner of Saint-Antoine and Berri—
the smallish brick apartment building with the apartment,
the one on the upper left,
the one with the windows surrounded by flower boxes.

Do you know it?
Throughout the summer,
maybe even the fall,
the flowers are so well maintained,
they surround the windows on all four sides.
Have you ever wondered
how they water the flower boxes above the windows?
You must have wondered.

You've seen it, I'm sure.
It's right on the bike path,
and right off the highway,
and the flowers look almost fake,
that's how beautiful they are.

Once upon a December,
Kayla and I walked out of our freshman dorm,
Furnald Hall at Columbia University,
and she remarked that the snowbound trees, so beautiful,
were like a winter-wonderland-themed bar mitzvah,
and I said, no, they're like
a winter wonderland.

I just want to know if you've seen the flowers,
and thought about them? Guillaume wants
to buy fake fruit for a pleasing fruit bowl I found,
so we can keep the fruit bowl in the living room,
and I said, sure, but then let's buy fake fruit
that's explicitly fake, purple lemons or somesuch.

They're not worth a detour, the flowers,
but if you're biking or driving by,
and you get the long red light to cross Saint-Antoine,
do look up awhile. There's nothing else
to see right there anyway and I'm pretty sure
they're real flowers. Have you ever seen
someone watering them?

In 2019, it seemed that everyone had dead plants
in their house, there were flower stores that sold
more dead flowers than living ones,
dyed, not garishly, but dyed all the same.
We had them too, at the time,
but then it started occurring to me,
with increasing frequency,
that they were dead.

I'd love to see the tenant watering their flowers.
Tell me if you see them first. That would be enough,
almost.

Storytelling

after "Golden Buzzer: Lavender Darcangelo wins over Heidi Klum with a STUNNING song! | Auditions | AGT 2023"

Lavender Darcangelo walks on stage in a lavender dress and beige ballet flats, guided by an older bald man in shades of khaki. He places her in the centre of the stage as she raises a microphone, prepared to interact with the judges. Howie Mandel goes first, asking "who do we have here?" and "who are you with?" and "how old are you?" and Lavender responds, confidently, that she is "Lavender" and she is with her "wonderful dad" and she is "twenty-seven years old." Howie's questions continue, and Lavender answers in kind, she'll be singing a song, she's been singing since she was three, singing before she could talk, she's autistic and blind, she has a lot of dreams, she wants to build a school where the classes are based off things kids are naturally curious about, a school she would have thrived in. Howie's attention turns more fully to the wonderful dad, whose name is Will, who adopted her later in life, she met him at an afterschool program, she gives Will the microphone, he started an afterschool music program, he and Lavender met, she asked him to adopt her, he was a member of the faculty and he couldn't or shouldn't but then Lavender was having struggles and so she moved in with Will and his husband Jamie—husband—the camera cuts to a man with silver hair and glasses and a horseshoe moustache and his eyes are glassy with tears and yours are too, that's odd, your eyes are glassy too, she moved in right after Will and Jamie's honeymoon and Will whispers some subtitled words of encouragement and she's getting ready to sing and the camera cuts to Jamie again and he says to the woman next to him "I can't believe my girl is on stage" and it's really happening now, the glass is coming off your eyes and falling down your face and you're heaving, your breath is gone, and Lavender is singing "Out Here on My Own" from *Fame* by Irene Cara—"Sometimes I wonder / where I've been / who I am / do I fit in?"—you're making noises now, from the throat or somewhere deeper, they wake your partner up and he's panicking, why are you sobbing in bed on a Tuesday at midnight, and you can't tell him why because you can't say the words "*America's Got Talent*" while you're in this state—

This is the story you tell your daughter: the story of the moment you knew you wanted, needed her. Or this is the story of a haunting: "I can't believe my girl is on stage" playing in your head as you buy cute toys for your friends' kids.

Dear Mr. and Mrs. Banu, please give this to your son, my new friend Rubin, 1933

Hello how lovely it was to have
met you, yesterday, I do so hope
our paths cross again, if not
at the company, although I do
so hope you are selected, and

I will, of course, put in as good
a word as I am able to put, but
if not, perhaps, a stroll along
the Dâmboviţa, or another place,
you can choose, or I can, perhaps

with, you didn't mention, do you
have a sweetheart, I do, her name
is, well, it doesn't matter now, and
if you don't have a sweetheart,
I won't bring mine, she can go

to the teahouse with her friends,
she likes that, she has some pretty
friends, perhaps one for you, but
first, a stroll, just you and me,
perhaps, to discuss the company,

if you are selected, or other companies,
if you are not, I know them all
quite well and would happily
make you know them and make
you know me and I know you

so that, should opportunities
arise, I would know you
to know
to tell
you of them.

Meet me by the bridge, I've decided,
the Podul Opereta, that's a place
I like to go,
to walk,
to talk.

Sienna

Four pillows on our bed
All with linen cases
The colour called sienna

Before he goes to sleep
He removes one sienna pillowcase
Replaces it with black cotton

To preserve the linen
Protect it from his night cream and
Occasional night drool

I first bought him the night cream
For Christmas
The brand is Australian

The linen is French
Just like the Grotte Chauvet
Site of famed cave paintings

Including three steppe lions
I had tattooed on my forearm
Two and a half years before I met him

Dozens of men touched the tattoo
Before he did
Including an Australian

But none ever rolled over
From some drool-encrusted black cotton
To gently kiss the lions

As the day's first act
Sienna was a clay-based pigment
Used by some Palaeolithic artist

Who didn't have pillowcases to change
Or pillows for that matter
Never would have spent the morning

Being asked by their lover
Whether ivory, white, or charcoal
Would work best

As an additional accent cushion
Before the artist's violent death
Trampled, gored, or bludgeoned

I hope he knew tenderness at dawn

Belongings IV

I'm trying, I really am, to do this research thing, I'm reading books and everything, and not just books I buy, library books, even if each page I turn is a reminder of how many dirty fingers have turned the pages before me, and by everything I also mean going to the Canadian Jewish Archives, going in person and everything, and by everything I mean sitting there for a couple hours and chatting with the kind experts and looking at the original copies of documents showing that I know even less about my great-grandfather than I thought I did and will most likely not know more, and by everything I mean following up with some genealogical wizard who's not getting back to me, and I'm this close to holding a seance, I want more knowledge and less wisdom, I can fabricate wisdom, can whip up a pithy and touching line, but I want to know, do you understand, I want to know things about people long dead and no, thank you kindly, but no, I don't want to apply for a travel grant, I don't want to sift through the singed records of a burned synagogue in a country that hates me for two reasons, if I wanted to go to a place that hates me I'd simply book a flight to Miami, my friend Lauren's parents have a lovely vacation home on Fisher Island, you have to take a private ferry to get there, but at least when I arrive on the dock I know I'm on the list.

The Limits of Fiction

In a hotel room in Burlington, Vermont, I try to get my grandfather to tell me if his parents ever told him stories about the old country, but he just wants to tell me about Lili St. Cyr at the Gayety.

Nobody wants to fuck me anymore.

It's just that I think I was taught that once you wear an engagement ring, everybody wants to fuck you all the time.

I'm worried I've made it all up. I'm worried that none of it really happened, is really happening.

Do these poems convey that I am, at my core, a good person?

I can't masturbate to fantasy. Fantasy is just disappointment, gussied up. If it's not going to happen, why would I think about it.

I'm worried it's not going to happen, for me.

I can imagine what happened in the old country, I've read enough books, seen enough movies. But what did a fingertip feel like, in the old country, grazing your palm? I imagine fingertips were rougher back then, bloodied from the cold. I could be so wrong. Their skin could have been so soft.

ERNEST ♥ KR(~~ubin~~)YSTYNA; or, A Whole Life

Ernest meets Krystyna at a place and in a way that people meet—maybe he knocks on her parents' door to sell them linens, maybe a mutual acquaintance fixes them up, maybe she catches his eye at a synagogue social—and they ~~kiss for the first time in a back room of the National Theatre in Bucharest, a kiss that could almost be called accidental, a kiss that starts when Ernest trips over some discarded rigging and falls into Rubin, his scruffy chin rubbing against Rubin's smooth cheek, which Rubin turns so his lips meet Ernest's nose, and then his mouth, and then their mouths are open, and the thing that Rubin and Krystyna have most in common is their serpentine tongues~~ marry after a courtship appropriate in its length and chasteness and they have a daughter named Margot and then a son named Isaac, Izzy for short, and then, a decade later, a daughter named Ruby, which is also her birthstone ~~and the English translation for the Romanian *rubin*, when *The Wizard of Oz* was released Ernest took Krystyna on a date to see it at the Théâtre Saint-Denis and he had to feign illness because the ruby slippers were just too much for him to take, both in their etymological impact and their beauty, Rubin would have loved them so much, he would have begged the company's costumer to make him a pair of ruby pointe shoes~~ and the house is full of something that is almost love, a cousin of it once removed, and Krystyna has her moments, she lies down on the kitchen floor with a butcher knife to her chest when the kids don't do their chores, and Ernest has his disappearances ~~using his whole palm to push a hustler's face against a flophouse pillow since the only thing the boy has in common with Rubin is the way his hair grows far down the nape of his neck~~ but Margot and Izzy and Ruby turn out all right and each meets an appropriate Jew of the appropriate gender and each has two to four children with names like Rachel, like Aaron, and Ernest ~~to an extent that feels to him perverse, thinks of Rubin not less and less as time does what time does but more and more~~ when remembered is remembered tenderly, he was quiet, he was kind, he was misunderstood, one of his children tells one of his great-grandchildren of her last memory of her father, of Ernest trying to take her hand the day before his surgery, she was sixteen, she's unsure if she let her hand be taken.

To Riches

Before she left the industry,
my mother once described herself
as a schmattologist:

a scholar of the rag.
Before they took her uterus,
she'd say she was on the rag
but she'd never call a pad a schmatta—

that's only cloth
or clothes, if ugly
or shapeless and used to
warm: "hand me that schmatta,"

which I'd like to say
when I need to wipe him off me,
but even though he's been made familiar

he wouldn't know
that, no, I don't just mean a Kleenex.

The Male Dancer

Billy Elliot was the first movie to make me cry from an emotion other than fear, but that was because, if I recall correctly, of dead mother content and not ballet content. I saw it in theatres; I would have been nine or ten.

On *Modern Family*, the straight actor who plays Cam, the flamboyant gay husband, does quite an amusing impression of Billy Elliot in a bad northern accent ("I just want to dance at the ballet") that later became somewhat of a meme.

The character of Billy is straight and the actor who plays him is straight too. But when men dance ballet, they're seen as gay, hence the film's central tension, other than the miners' strike.

I learned the term "scab" from *Billy Elliot*, that I remember very clearly.

I do think I always wanted to dance at the ballet. The memory of the desire is vague, foggy.

Once, I asked my friend Erin to confirm that she was there when I told the assistant principal of our high school that someone had scratched "FAG" into my locker. She was, she remembered. The scene felt like something I had seen in a movie, so I was worried I had made it up.

I have recurrent pain in my feet. I went to see a podiatrist, Dr. Bluma Girzon. She took X-rays and I was flattered when she told me I should have been a ballet dancer because of my very high arches, which also put added pressure on my heels and the balls of my feet when I wear thin-soled shoes.

I went to a few ballet classes with Rosalie, my fiancé's cousin. They were actually ballet-barre workout classes. I think one of the teachers told me I was a natural, but I could really just be making that up. Anyway, I found the barre elements a bit too strenuous.

I find male ballet dancers to be attractive, generally, by which I mean I like the body type imposed upon them by the rigours of the form and also by troubling aesthetic expectations and codes. But there's something deeply unerotic about seeing them on stage, possibly because of the false, Ken-like modesty of their dance belts.

When my great-aunt Cynthia told me that her father danced ballet before fleeing Romania, I made some immediate assumptions about him, assumptions that were somewhat bolstered by other knowledge I had, like that he was less successful in business than some of his peers.

Cynthia, whom I call Yaya, probably said that she *thought* her father danced ballet before *leaving* Romania.

In CEGEP, we had to write and perform a short two-person play. I insisted that Tiffany and I wear matching black tights, which I bought using our mutual friend Lauren's employee discount at American Apparel, even though tights weren't remotely essential to our characters.

My parents put me on a soccer team when I was a child, then took me off it when I did nothing but wander around the field snapping my fingers. They put me in karate, chess, piano. They never forced me to continue any of the activities I didn't like, which was all of them. But they never put me in ballet. I never asked.

My legs look good in tights. My mother always says I have better legs than either she or my father has. Maybe they're my great-grandfather's legs. Maybe, just like me, he never even danced.

THIS ISN'T A GAY POEM.

I'm gay, but this poem isn't.

This poem will talk about gay things, but if you say it's a gay poem, that's offensive.

If you comment on this poem, please be gay, but also if you don't comment on this poem, and you're not gay, you're a homophobe.

This poem will talk about coming out, and how I'm always having to come out, and how when I came out to my mother she said "as long as you're getting your dick sucked," but this isn't a poem about coming out.

This poem will talk about my mother, in a way many gay men do, but my talking about my mother is unrelated to this gay corpus, even though my mother made me gay.

If you read this poem and think my mother made me gay, you're archaic, but if you don't believe me when I tell you my mother made me gay, you're denying my agency.

This poem will fuck you in the ass and then make you suck your shit off its dick, but that doesn't make it gay, and, don't worry, it doesn't make you gay either.

This poem will use faggot with abandon, but when you read the poem, don't say faggot, not even in your head, just clench your sphincter and move along, like some kind of fucking faggot.

This poem will tell you, in its tender moments, that someone scratched "FAG" into my locker in high school, and that will make you feel better about all the "faggots." This poem will then push you up against that locker, its throbbing cock ready for round two, and ask you why you needed me to be damaged to feel comfortable.

This poem will be campy and flouncy and fey, this poem will be leather and poppers and latex, this poem will own two tiny poodles named Judy and Liza, and they're both gay, but this poem isn't.

Relate to this poem, but don't call it relatable. Recognize its universality, but know it's not universal. Accept this poem as a gift, even though it's not for you, breeder scum.

This poem is begging you to milk its prostate.

This poem chooses not to be gay.

Ernest Wonders

Conjecture	Catalyst
After Ernest left, Rubin was overcome with grief and regret. He changed his mind and, quickly, he too found his way to transatlantic escape. But the ship sank and Rubin drowned.	A sweltering summer day. Ernest's daughter wants to play tea party at the bottom of the pool. She stays a moment too long and there's panic in her limbs as she thrusts toward the surface.
After Ernest left, Rubin was overcome with jealousy and regret. He changed his mind and, quickly, he too found his way to transatlantic escape. Made it to Montreal, where he lives a life just parallel to Ernest's, delicately avoiding him, occasionally taunting him.	Ernest's car breaks down and he has to take the streetcar. It's empty, save for its stoic driver. Ernest walks to the back of the car, where he's hit by an odour, familiar in its strangeness, appealing in its hint of the stables. It's the smell of Rubin's perineum, he's sure of it.
Rubin was rounded up, sent to a camp: Bogdanovka, maybe. Got typhus and died. Gassed. Shot in the head. Torn apart by dogs. Hypothermia. Burned alive.	This is the norm. The soundtrack to Ernest's life. His equilibrium, occasionally punctuated by other thoughts. A parasite he's grown to love. Tinnitus he'd rather leave untreated.

Conjecture	**Catalyst**
Rubin was rounded up, sent to a camp. There, his pillowy lips caught the attention of a guard. Sex as protection, as currency. Sex as saviour. The war ended and they fled to Buenos Aires together. They live there happily, and every night before bed, Rubin promises himself he'll smother Fritz in his sleep.	The cover of one of Krystyna's tawdry Harlequins, some busty blonde held wilfully captive by a man in epaulets.
Rubin survived Ernest's leaving, survived the camps, the beatings, the post-war bleakness, survived being alive, survives still or doesn't, is or was just perfectly fine.	Most days, life is liveable. The children smile.
After Ernest left, Rubin made himself a cup of coffee. Took a long walk along the Dâmbovița. After Ernest left, Rubin was overcome with relief.	Ernest takes Krystyna and the kids to the beach in Wildwood, New Jersey. He looks across the Atlantic and nothing looks familiar, feels familiar. He can't even picture the other side.

Postmodernity Is of Course a Euphemism for Internalized Homophobia

In 1971, my grandfather bought a country house in Morin-Heights that came with a ceramic statue of a turquoise unicorn. The unicorn is at rest, legs folded underneath itself, nestled on some clouds. Or, not quite at rest, but posing, its head held high and its chin tucked in to its chest, its twisted horn perpendicular to its brow, to its snout. The unicorn has a luscious mane, hair piled high as a shiny pompadour on an Elvis Presley wax figure. The unicorn's ass is surprisingly human and shockingly well defined, two juicy cheeks beneath a tiny tufted tail. The unicorn is covered with a pattern of textureless cracks, so smooth and regular that they appear superimposed, a filter.

This effect is an example of crackle, the technique by which a spiderweb of fine cracks is created in a ceramic glaze. Crackle is distinct from crazing, which is the same thing, but by mistake. The answer to an old-fashioned SAT analogy question would read "manslaughter is to murder as crazing is to crackle." Maybe the cracks are in fact an example of crazing, and maybe the statue was left behind in the Laurentian chalet because of its defect, or maybe it was left behind without forethought.

In the five decades since my grandfather accidentally acquired the ceramic statue of a turquoise unicorn, unicorns have become gay. In the five decades since my grandfather accidentally acquired the ceramic statue of a turquoise unicorn, I have both become gay and acquired the ceramic statue of a turquoise unicorn. This unicorn lives in the home I share with my gay fiancé.

I hesitated before acquiring the ceramic statue of a turquoise unicorn, before accepting my parents' offer to have it fill a previously unfilled corner in our apartment. I hesitated because intention is difficult to express in interior design without a plaque that reads "we are gay but this unicorn is not." I hesitated because one of the many curses of postmodernity is a refusal to be on the nose.

They removed analogies from the SAT, but I'm only comfortable with crazing. Manslaughter carries a lesser sentence.

Our Man Rubin

Rubin was my best friend
when we were children and our
fathers were best friends before us,
we lost touch when he left our hometown.
Years later, in the camp, I thought I saw
him with a pickaxe slung over his shoulder
and I nearly guffawed, Rubin always
seemed so ill-equipped for labour,
but I thought I saw a lot of
things back then.

Rubin was kind to me.
Once, he made me a jam.
Or bought it.
I don't remember if
the jam was good.

Rubin took me in the French
fashion, a few times, behind the yeshiva.
He was known as the resident peter-eater
and he was quite good at it. I remember
being touched, almost, how deeply he
seemed to breathe me in when his nose
rested in my pubic hair. I wondered
if he did that for all the boys.

My Rubeleh came out of
his mother dancing, I always
said, and she tried so hard to get
him to stop that he left. I went to see
him once, told his mother I was going
to visit an ailing uncle. I couldn't
believe my boy was on stage. I
couldn't believe he couldn't
know I was there.

Rubin would do this thing that never failed to reduce me to hysterics. We'd be sharing a meal, just the two of us or with friends, or even acquaintances, and he would, in the middle of conversation, usually mercifully in the middle of a long-winded story, smear food across his entire face and then ask if he could borrow someone's handkerchief.

Rubin was the most technically gifted dancer we ever had but he was incapable, or unwilling, of moving around the stage in a way befitting of a man.

Rubin loved me very deeply, I knew, but I loved my wife, or at least my sons, and he was a kike, to boot.

Rubin sighed when he came, melodically, a whistle, almost, like a small mammal being squeezed too hard or just hard enough, you can never be sure, is this pain or pleasure? I always got the sense Rubin knew the difference, knew where to draw the line, but chose to keep that distinction a secret.

Analytic Frameworks

The thing about Jews is, we're obsessed with Persian rugs, but sometimes our parents call them by a name that's no longer acceptable. I even knew a Jew who had his housekeeper help him switch out his Persian rugs every season. Fall is just around the corner and now would be the time he would be forcing a petite woman to help him shove an unwieldy spiral into the elevator of a past-its-prime-but-still-aristocratic building on Atwater. He was a Jew from the Maritimes, which is a weird place to be a Jew from, in theory, but, in practice, is closer to Europe than non-Maritime provinces are. He was a homosexual octogenarian Jew, when I knew him, and a homosexual Jew before I knew him. Once I tried to engage him on the novels of Edmund White but he wasn't interested. Once I asked him lots of questions about the dill pickle soup he had his Filipina housekeeper prepare based on his Polish bubby's recipe and he was very interested in that. His bubby was a hard woman, deeply lined by forty-five, who got out of Poland before the getting was direr, who showed him little kindness other than to make him the zupa ogórkowa she knew he loved whenever he would visit. He was a dear friend of my mother's late mother, whom I never knew. I've never referred to anyone as a dear friend but people did once, I figure, back when they were friends. I wonder if she called him in a panic when "Rare Cancer Seen in 41 Homosexuals" dropped in the *Times* in 1981. I wonder if she would have had she not been dying of a common cancer. I wonder if she would have told him to be careful, and I wonder if he would have brushed her off. I wonder if she would have called him when I started asking for Swarovski crystal animals for birthdays and for Hanukkah. I'd wonder less if he had engaged with me on the novels of Edmund White.

In college I had a fake Persian rug, a cheap runner my father Amazon Prime'd me when I told him that my friends and lovers complained that my room resembled a cell. I woke up in the middle of one night and vomited into my trash but in the morning realized it wasn't my trash it was the Amazon rug and I was late to teach public speaking and debate to students at an underserved Manhattan public school or for a Mandarin quiz and so I ran out of my room and it wasn't until I got back late that night that I remembered the vomit I had left and so I wrapped up the rug like a vomit burrito and threw it directly down the trash chute.

I've lied about the friends and lovers. I brought but two lovers back to that room, and neither cared to comment on its sparseness.

I've lied about the Polish bubby and her dill pickle soup. I have no recollection of what he said to me about the soup. He talked about it at length, but I was preoccupied by the novels of Edmund White.

Ernest Dances Siegfried in *Swan Lake*

after Ernst Wilhelm Lotz's "The Dancer," translated by Alexandra Kolb

There's a moment in the grand adage:
Siegfried lifts Odette above his head
vision obscured by layers of tulle
his hands grip ribs and could those ribs
not be his lover's?

And his lover, watching below,
staring upward, feels his torso
pressed by sturdy hands.

And they discover, as fortunate others
have before, that when two lovers dream
in unison the world for once spins kindly,

an alteration of the poles' magnetic
pull, a proof that naught can't be the source nor
purpose of all this, one lover's hands upon
another's ribs, in flagrant dereliction of
the horror known as truth.

Two lovers dance the "Love Duet"
for a rapt audience
who will never know
this trick of happenstance,

save for one wide-eyed girl
who'll find it out when she and her lover
dream of ice lollies on a scorching
August night, both women wake up
sweet and cool
with tacky tongues.

(Help Me Choose a Photo of) My Engagement Ring (to Post on Instagram)

Photo 1

Description*:* A white hand emerges from the bottom of the frame, where a few dark wrist hairs are visible. The hand has five digits: four fingers and a thumb. Below the second knuckle of the second longest finger, the ring finger, sits, in fact, a ring. The setting of the ring is a matte gold disc and from the disc emerge six sets of prongs, each holding one of six gems: three red, one green, one purple, and one yellow. The red gems are very small, the green gem is somewhat small and sparkles most, the purple gem is roughly hewn, and the yellow gem is star-shaped. Just under the ring, a few dark finger hairs are visible. The ring, by local queer designer Alexandre Bergeron, attempts to distract from the unmade bed in the background of the image. The bed's sheets, by French brand Carré Blanc but purchased locally, are red, but more sienna than the cherry of the three small gems.

Analysis: The ring is clearly visible and transparently made visible, but there's a certain candidness in the position of my fingers, in the messiness of the bed. I'm showing off the ring, to be sure, but I'm also just living my life. What a surprise, the photo seems to say, I didn't even have the chance to ask my now-fiancé to make the bed or shave my knuckles. An important caveat: in this photo, the ring is on my right hand. Neither I nor the man who gave me the ring realized that engagement rings are meant to be worn on the left hand until a few female friends remarked on the error.

Photo 2

Description: The aforementioned hand with the aforedescribed ring lies flat on a black table, the tips of its fingers holding open a greeting card from local stationery producer Paperole. The left side of the greeting card is blank but on the right side is a note written in purple ink: "Misha, / Cette année, tout l'amour que je veux t'exprimer tient dans une petite phrase. Et dans une petite boîte... / Guillaume."

Analysis: The ring is still on the wrong hand here and my gay fiancé Guillaume has asked that I stop sharing his intimate words publicly. It's a bit much, perhaps, to share the note that accompanied the proposal, but is it not also deeply humanizing? My mostly straight, mostly progressive followers do so adore gay love, and even my most ardently anti-marriage followers, of which there are approximately none, would surely be touched by such a pure evocation. Isn't Millennial irony out in favour of renewed youthful earnestness? And how earnest, we two men in love, neither socialized to dream of rings, neither knowing where to put one. We're queering homonormativity, don't you see? This is radical, especially because I'm a top and we hardly have penetrative sex.

Photo 3

Description: In the crisp foreground, the mirror image of the previous hand now wears the ring. In the blurry background sits a small black dog, a Shorkie from Puppy Country in nearby Saint-Rémi, who seems to be looking at the hand. The dog is seated on a black cushion and a few brightly coloured dog toys are strewn about the floor.

Analysis: The ring is now on the correct hand. The inclusion of my puppy is a strategic win: the only thing my followers love more than gay love is dogs. We've done away with the overt posing of the second option in favour a more natural background akin to the first option. My concern is the lack of narrative heft; the photo captures neither my genuine surprise and elation nor the rapidity with which I said "oui." Yes, I was truly surprised! What's that? Why did he have to do the asking? Why couldn't this have been decided jointly? Why are we recreating patterns we swore to swear off? Listen, I bet you didn't even know the thumb isn't a finger.

Heidi and Marcia and Mary and Cynthia

Heidi is my mother, she dyes her hair red.

Marcia was my grandmother, she dyed her hair red,
then lost her hair, and then my grandfather bought her
an expensive Hasidic wig.

Mary was my great-grandmother, she dyed her hair
red, slept every night on a silk doughnut-shaped pillow.

Mary died in the bath when I was fourteen. Before that, we
had brunch every Sunday at Snowdon Deli with Heidi. Once,
we saw a woman she knew. After, in the car, she told a story
about how that woman's then-dead husband always
carried his wife's purse around for her.

Marcia died six years before I was born. We would have loved
each other, I've been told. Once, I had a dream that she had
been in quarantine all this time, waiting to be let out of a bunker.

Heidi is alive, but talks about death a lot.

We would have loved each other, I've been told.

Heidi lost a brother at ten, a mother at twenty-one, three
fetuses after I was born.

"What, was her pussy made of gold?" is the punchline
of the story Mary told. I've been told I rely too much on
punchlines. Punchlines are the end of a joke, and therefore
its death. What I really rely on is death, here it is, take it in,
feel it in your DNA.

Here's another one: when I came out to Heidi, she said "as long as you're getting your dick sucked!"

I don't have a punchline about Marcia, but Heidi surely would.

Cynthia is Mary's daughter, Marcia's sister, Heidi's aunt. Cynthia is my great-aunt, she dyes her hair blonde.

Once, Cynthia rubbed my tummy while I struggled on the toilet. She told me that her father danced ballet back in Romania.

Cynthia's father died when she was sixteen. The next day, a large skin discolouration appeared on her back, like she had been sucker-punched.

Punched, punchline. I don't get it either.

What Krystyna Knew

Krystyna knew she needed a soft man to let her dreams come true

Krystyna knew enough feygeles from working at her sister's dress shop to know her husband was one

Krystyna knew Ernest would never leave her

Krystyna knew Ernest would never love her

Krystyna knew Ernest would never raise a hand to their children

Krystyna knew Ernest would never come home drunk and sob to his twelve-year-old daughter that he wished her mother still looked like her

Krystyna knew that sex was easy to find

Krystyna knew where he went at night

Krystyna knew he was still a man, knew to lie about where she went at night

Krystyna knew she'd own the finest dress shop in Montreal

Krystyna knew Miss Clairol Hair Color Bath in Copper Tone was the key to the goyim

Krystyna knew not to correct men when they spelled her name Christina

Krystyna knew not to correct men

Krystyna knew her husband was made of porcelain and covered in cracks

Krystyna knew the wrong gust of wind would reduce him to shards

Krystyna knew one day she'd fill her cheeks and blow

Krystyna knew, yes, Krystyna knew Ernest

Julia Writes to Say

she "just ate the best god damn nectarine"

"of [her] life."

She clarifies for the group chat,
which includes her twin sister and my first cousin,
that a decade ago I told her the best thing in life
was a cold, crisp nectarine.

I don't remember telling her exactly that,
but I remember the era in which I would have said something like it,
more than a decade ago, in fact, when nectarines were still free
(bought and washed and served by a parent)
and I hadn't yet cum inside of someone I love.

Back then we told each other lots of things
(we swore to be each other's confidants)—
she had boy problems and boy successes
and I, I guess, had nectarines.

Now she lives on the opposite coast of another country—
last time I was there my boy and I met hers.
Sometimes, out of the blue, she writes me with a secret.

There was a time she knew me better,
better than she does now,
better than those who know or have known me
by my smell, the feeling of my skin, the sound of my voice,
the sound of my heartbeat, the gurgling of my stomach, my breath
in their ear, my ear in their mouth, my head in their lap, my lap
on their face, by my face, my face
close to theirs and then turned away—
but there's no better way to be known
than in the mouthfeel of a stonefruit.

Yesterday Down at the Canal

after Frank O'Hara

September heat is worse
than July heat or better
if you're hoping for it

but if you're not hoping for it
it's definitely worse and my little dog
pants and pants his pink tongue over
his crooked teeth his thick body
swaying, woozy like the hazy air

you tell me I should appreciate the water
you tell me it's beautiful here, to live here
but I can't jump in to cool off and the sun
makes me squint makes me sweat makes me
press my eyes closed behind my sunglasses
so how should I even see it

I want to love life
I want to love my life I want
so much of everything I want my little dog
curled up next to me I want to feel
his fur I want him to have never been born
I want an endless summer I want the heat to end
I want to live forever I want the world to end

I pull my dog away from another dog's shit
I step in a third dog's shit

when I get home I'll throw away my sandals
you'd tell me I was being silly
you'd tell me you could wash them for me
I did like these sandals up until just now but
things can change in an instant and it turns out
maybe I want so much less, so much less
of it

THIS IS A POLITICAL POEM.

I don't write about politics, apart from all my writing being political because of gay, and maybe because of Jewish, but rest assured I believe in all the same progressive causes as you do. I don't mean to be flippant about it, but I just know we're on the same page and I don't feel I have anything to add to the conversation, at least nothing that wouldn't centre me in places, things, ideas I shouldn't be central in or to.

I'd like to tell you, I guess, that twice in the past year men have stage-whispered "ça sent le fif icitte," it smells like faggot here, as my fiancé and I have walked by. I just think you should be aware.

Once I'm at it, I'd also take this opportunity to tell you that I do have a solution to this problem: the solution is violence. Violence is the answer. You see, if in response to "ça sent le fif icitte," I could have confidently beat the shit out of the men, caused a zygomatic fracture and the like, the problem would be solved, at least on my end. I can't think of an alternate solution. Education, sure, but that ship has sailed. "Excuse me, sirs," I could have said, "have you ever thought about the power of your words? I'm just calling you in, would you be interested in having a conversation about acceptance?" Unsatisfying and dangerous.

Another solution I've considered is responding to a slur with an insult, really cutting them down to size, but most insults are classist in some way, or about the body, and I'm not trying to cause more harm. Well, I would like to cause harm, but only to these men, not to any cause, and I would really like the harm to be physical.

Violence might be the answer for them, too, to really put the phobia in homophobia. "Stay away from faggots," the men would whisper in their men circles, "they can really pack a punch." Yes, this is my platform, as it were. This is what I have to offer. I'll start by looking up "boxing classes near me queer-friendly gym."

The House on Circle Road

I barely remember the house, but I cried when I left it,
can recall an antique mirror on the floor,
a flacon with my name on the side:

a perfume by the Russian dancer who shares my name—
my name, *my* name, a name isn't owned.
My parents owned that house and that house alone.

They rented, they rent, I rent still.
I know more about the house than I remember,
as if it were the site of a famed battle:

The Plains of Abraham, the house in which my bris was held.
What it could have offered: the raspberry bushes,
the stairs, how I long for stairs.

Stairs are possibility, a suggestion of more—
in a house you don't always know what's up
or down, you get that boxed-cat

mystery—that's what I want, to know
less, to wonder more—a life without stairs
is a life unowned—to own is to wonder:

"is this really mine?"—instead of knowing:
"no it isn't, nothing
ever is."

Three Sonnets About the Art in My Home

Inherited Painting by Unknown Artist

She's looking at a painting by some old Italian master, hung
in a gilded frame upon a blue-grey wall, her leg outstretched
as if to balance the weight of her consideration. Towards me
another painting: a landscape, maybe, vivid colours; to her right
a large and temporary wall—another exhibit not yet ready. I've seen
her in a photo, a design magazine from the 80s, a feature on my
grandfather's cabin, the largest all-wood cabin in Canada
at the time. She was, for a while, under my single guest bed, now
she's on my double-occupancy wall. She lived in a cabin I've visited
pre-memory, so finds repugnant my nostalgia, her hip cocked
mockingly. But she can never access the incomplete exhibit, stuck
looking at some Jesus in his vermillion robes. She was bought
with money we'll never see the likes of: we spent our final paycheque
on the garish entry fee, only to find the cabin sold, the museum half-closed.

Gifted Painting by Louise Scott

The painting's frame was originally more baroque but Guillaume didn't
like it so my father offered to spray paint it off-white. I liked
the gaudy gold frame but Guillaume already didn't like
the art itself and love is compromise.
My mother's dead mother's dead gay friend
gave me this painting for my bar mitzvah
(he was alive then). In every upper-middle-class Jewish home
in Montreal you'll find a similar painting, moonfaced figures
with Mona Lisa eyes at a carnival or vaguely medieval or lounging
on a chaise or, at my parents' upper duplex, getting married.
I have a fiancé who has a foreskin and there's no middle class anymore
and so my walls need this painting or they're not mine. Self-love
is also compromise: I tell myself it's a painting but it's really
just a print.

Thrifted Milk Jug by Unknown Artist

A solitary figure, pink, let's call him a man,
sits and fishes beneath a large pink umbrella.
Across the blue pond: green trees, blue clouds, pink sky.
The man in the milk jug art puts down
his rod, his umbrella, turns to me, says
"hey man do you want a blow job?"
My partner and I bought this decorative
milk jug together, in a church basement
antique sale, not at a charming
small-town church basement antique sale,
at a reductive Mile-End one, but we loved
the colours and now, look at me, I'm balls
deep in this fisherman and it turns out those weren't clouds
across the pond, they were further trees, shadowed blue.

History of the Jews in Quebec

It was time to move to Hampstead
or Côte Saint-Luc
or Snowdon
or even Chomedey
on that other island north of this one,
but it was time to move.

Krystyna found the house,
Ernest found the money,
the kids would find new friends
or wouldn't need to—
the old ones were moving too
or had already moved.

Move move move move—
Ernest always moving,
years since he had moved
the way he used to move
on stage, years of simply moving
West.

Now at least moving toward
instead of just away.
A bigger house, a bigger
lawn, a memory: he and Krystyna
moving into their first
apartment together, realizing

in tandem that it was their only
home, remembering their parents'
homes, remembering they were
burnt or razed, remembering their parents,
remembering—better not to remember
all that much.

Their children and their children's
children still live in Hampstead and
Côte Saint-Luc and Snowdon, but
not Chomedey, that's all Greek. Unless
they live in Toronto. Their children's children's children
live in neighbourhoods like Little Burgundy,

in places like converted steel factories
surrounded by things like murals of jazz greats,
remembering, or trying not to, that different
people lived here before they did.
And I'd like to read more about that,
in someone else's poem.

The Seafood Buffet at Boca West Country Club, c. 1998–2010

There were people whose job it was to shake the lobster flesh
out of the lobster claws. You'd go up to their station and ask
for six claws and they'd break the claws off three steamed
lobsters and throw the remaining carcasses into a pile
for those who wanted tail meat, presumably, or for
those older Jews who, raised by survivors or
survivors themselves, found pleasure
in scraping the torsos and savouring
the tomalley, the greenish-
brown organ
mush.

But some
lobster bodies
must have gone to
waste, the extremities
were so much more popular
than the interiors. Maybe they
made for an impromptu staff meal,
maybe the lobster crackers, all men,
mostly Eastern European, used the leftover
meat and prepared ramekins of melted butter
to woo nineteen-year-old white South African waitresses.

But you didn't think too much about that, you just held out your preheated plate and accepted six lopsided V's of white-and-red meat and wondered if you'd make it a dozen by the end of the night or save room for shrimp cocktail and molten lava cake.

And you did this at ten and eleven and twelve and so on, childhood and adolescence punctuated by seafood buffets, punch-drunk on privilege and too inured to it to criticize, an annual decadence you never knew would end.

And then it did, because someone paid for those lobsters, paid so much he can hardly afford his mostly publicly funded nursing home, so it's been a decade since your last buffet, and all you want to know is, can you be nostalgic for something that never should have been?

Time Travel

If I go back ninety years, say before my mother's mother's mother left Poland, I'm dead, in a camp or in a gleaming pile of shattered glass, and if I go back forty years, say before my mother's mother died of breast cancer, I'm dead, but boy do I dance before I go, and if I go back ten years I find myself, room 526 in Furnald Hall, and I take my thinner face between my slightly older hands I kiss myself for just so long that we both go forward all the years we could have would have lost.

I Try to Get My Grandfather to Tell Me Things His Parents Told Him

He tells me instead about Lili St. Cyr at the Gayety
whose burlesque act was Montreal's hottest ticket
and the clergy's cause célèbre.
Lili St. Cyr was born Marie Frances Van Schaack in Minneapolis, Minnesota
she began to dance professionally in a chorus line
she was known for quality, a high-class performer
all this is freely available on Wikipedia
laid bare, no need for a tasselled reveal
but I don't know where my grandfather's father was born
or why his mother's name was spelled Dory's
pronounced Doris, but with an apostrophe suggesting
ownership, contraction, turning away.
I know that my grandfather was born in Montreal and lived here
all his life, save for a stint in Laval, I know he went to Spain
right after high school and saw the bulls, I know
he had a hockey coach who was known to be a creep, I know
he owned a dress company, I know he lost a son, I know
last year he wanted to give away his son's jean jacket,
a child's jacket from the 70s, the biggest size his son ever wore, he kept it
for decades but just couldn't look at it anymore, I know
my mother took the jacket and it's in her closet, I know
he met Wayne Gretzky, Jay Leno, Jean Chrétien, I know
because he has photos stuck to the walls of his nursing home apartment.
As he gave my fiancé a tour of his photo walls, he got to a photo
of his son and said "he was only fourteen" and wailed for a moment, a true wail,
from the pit of his stomach, one solitary wail, and then he was back
to ski trips and country homes and the cheetah
he somehow rented for his son's bar mitzvah, back to emblems of a life
well lived, too well lived to be able to keep living well, and I want
to follow that wail back to its source, to that first primal wail
when the doctor spanked his tushy after he came out of Dory's, ride that wail
back through history and across an ocean, I want that wail

to serve as the opening note of my own little theatrical revue
where all my dead come out and dance to the tune of their mothers' lullabies
and end their act by peeling off one glove—they're wearing gloves, I didn't
mention that—stretching out their hands to me
so I can touch their skin and see if it feels like my own skin or somehow
very different, rougher, perhaps, or maybe smoother, a chorus line
of genealogy. I'm sure Lili St. Cyr put on a fabulous
show. I wish I could have seen it. It's just that burlesque
is still freely available, a ticket away, but all my other grandparents
are dead, and the last time I saw my grandfather it took him a second

before he knew me.

Our Father

Our father is a good daddy
Our father makes us eggs on the weekend
Our father goes away sometimes
Our father left a simple will
Our father smiles after he yells
Our father was a man of his time
Our father was a man out of time, if we think about it
Our father always holds our hands
Our father always wanted to hold our hands
Our father is nicer than our mother
Our father is sillier than our mother
Our father needed our mother more than she needed him
Our father takes us out for Chinese food when our mother says she needs a break
Our father makes money at his job
Our father was never good at making a living
Our father doesn't laugh a lot but it's a big one when he does
Our father has really shiny eyes
Our father is dead
One of us is dead, too
Two of us don't speak
Our father always says to be nice to each other
Our father has a different way of walking than the other fathers
Our father never met our children
Our father says he's proud of us
Our father would be proud of us, we hope
Our father wasn't clear about what made him proud
Our father had a name that wasn't his name
Our father has a funny name
Our father smelled like peppercorns, we think

Music

after Frank O'Hara

The tree just outside needs trimming
but in the meantime a big squirrel eats berries
by our open window
                    separated from the indoors by a metal screen.
Its clawing, its gnawing, sometimes its squeaks and barks
and breathy grunts, when it's talking to another squirrel.

Soon enough, fall, and no more berries,
the squirrel to where it goes in winter, the melting show,
the buds, the tree left uncut, the squirrel.

A hundred thousand million squirrels and one lives here
                                        and I do too.
My footsteps, my cracked knuckles, my curses, my blessings,
my moans. Soon enough, fall, my greying hair,
and nowhere to go but stay for winter.

I'm a hole / I'm a pole / My great-grandmother was a Pole

my eyes are holes / my pores are holes / my asshole is a hole
my arms are poles / my toes are poles / my nose is a pole with two holes
my great-grandmother left Poland in 1920-something / my great-grandmother was
three years old / my great-grandmother always said she was born in Warsaw
but we know that was a lie it was some shtetl

my mouth is a hole / my ears are holes / I'd die if you added another big enough hole
my fingers are poles / my legs are poles / yes fine my cock is a pole with one hole
my great-grandmother owned a dress shop / my great-grandmother would have died
in Poland / my great-grandmother died here and I've never been to Poland

my want is a hole / my need is a hole / my therapy is a hole disguised as a pole
my nipples are poles in the cold / my love is a pole and a hole / sometimes I can be
the perfect pole
my great-grandmother had holes and poles / my great-grandmother's parents had
holes and poles / I wonder if during a transatlantic escape from pogroms and
the like my great-grandmother's parents' holes were so deep there was relief to
be found in seeing them inversely / that is as poles

THIS IS A CULTURALLY JEWISH POEM.

Somewhere far across the sea
There is a place, it's nisht for me.
They say for feygeles it's great—
How fun! Let's set a wedding date.

I look for just a bissel meaning,
From my diasporic leanings;
I'm godless! HaShem only haunts
My poor and naked little schvantz.

Little? For a Heeb, my petzl's thick—
But that's enough about my dick.
I'd rather tell you of my bris,
Than all this fakakta tsuris.

I wish that I could tell you plain:
I'm really in a lot of pain.
Deep down I know that I'm a Jew,
But what that means I have no clue.

My mother calls me quite a bit?
My father's prone to ranting fits?
Bar mitzvah? Kugel? Holocaust?
Ancestry displaced and lost?

The irony in all my phrases?
The guilt I've felt through all my phases?
My upset stomach, diarrhea?
Chicken soup as panacea?

Shalom welcome to my Borscht Belt show!
Take my wife, please, I'm a homo!
I kid! I joke! I josh! I'm bored—
Identity as shield and sword.

I haven't been to shul in years,
But sometimes ringing in my ears,
I hear organ, I hear shofar—
I still ping on Chabad sonar,

And I'm flattered when they hand me
Lulav, etrog, beef salami.
Sorry, that last one's not hasid.
Can I tell you, Yid to Yid—

My thoughts on this are quite unkempt.
I'm stuck on stage, I'm all verklempt.
Please strike the gong, please cut me short,
I'm haunting this Catskills resort.

I am the Phantom of the Chosen!
My spiritual account is frozen
Until I pay a hefty fee
But it's unclear which currency

Would serve to have my name written
In the Book of Life, so bitte
Tell me what I owe this culture
So as not to be a vulture

Afeast on corpses unembalmed—
I'd like my guilty conscience calmed.
I write out "gee oh dee" in full
No dashing punches do I pull.

Seven digits indeed slaughtered—
Now become my writing fodder?
Do you think I'm less than staunch
When I say no people has carte blanche?

I want to find the means to mourn
Productively, to blow the horn
On some new tribe spread there and here
A Rosh that goes beyond the year,

Beyond ourselves and our mishegoss,
Beyond my navel, beyond loss.
Tikkun Olam! The nice Jews say—
Through that they find a better way

To be a Jew—and good for them.
I do agree, but I'm condemned
To find an answer just for me.
(Sorry to community.)

I thought I found it once of late
In the eyes of my beforeskinned mate
As he held out his emptied dish
And asked for more gefilte fish.

Meditations in an Emergency

after Frank O'Hara

Am I to bring a child into this world? Or find one in the world already?

Each time I look at a screen something new is aflame (sometimes the screen itself), but maybe that's how people used to feel upon unrolling their morning paper.

Why should I starve myself of this? Why don't I take a forkful of someone else's lavish cake?

I am the greatest father who never lived. All I do is sit around and wait to take my child to their activity.

Even trees mock me! Good heavens, I'm allergic to their gametes, aren't I? I'm just attacked by breeding every time I leave the house.

However, I have never tried to let myself be germinated by a tree. To hold in the sneeze so that the pollen can find some flower deep within my guts and make a sapling. A tree is slow to grow: I could live my life and then, when I am ready to depart, the crossbreed could erupt. I'd get to live forever, my skull perched upon my child's topmost crown of branches. And I'd be dead, so I'd never have to worry about all the burning.

The thing is I could save them but I don't

The thing is Ernest could grow old
spoil his grandchildren
come out at a ripe old age
find love

The thing is he could live so long
meet his great-grandson
know right away
just before he dies tell him
"don't make the same mistake I did"

There's no need for mistakes, is the thing
just before he dies could tell his great-grandson
"you'll be fine"
but the twinkle in his eye
could tell the younger man
everything he needs to know

Rubin could survive the camp
end up in Phoenix, Arizona
teach dance to kids with special needs
he and Ernest, the thing is, could write letters
talk on the phone, visit once a year
retire together, buy a bed and breakfast
make up for lost time

No time needs to be lost, time is only found
they could be reunited right away
life wouldn't easy but they'd have each other
the thing is, life could be easy
they'd have each other

Maybe there could be no camps
six million living, thriving, being, thinging
Ernest and Rubin: the biggest stars
Romanian ballet has ever seen
make love daily in their big plush bed
die holding hands at ninety-six

It's not true, is the thing:
fiction stranger than truth
queerer than truth
but also, and I'm sorry to ask you this,
what is truth?

The thing is happy endings mean I'm never born
but maybe I could write a collection of poems about my intergenerational—
what is the opposite of trauma?

The thing is everybody in my family is Jewish but nobody is gay
All I know is—my great-grandfather danced ballet

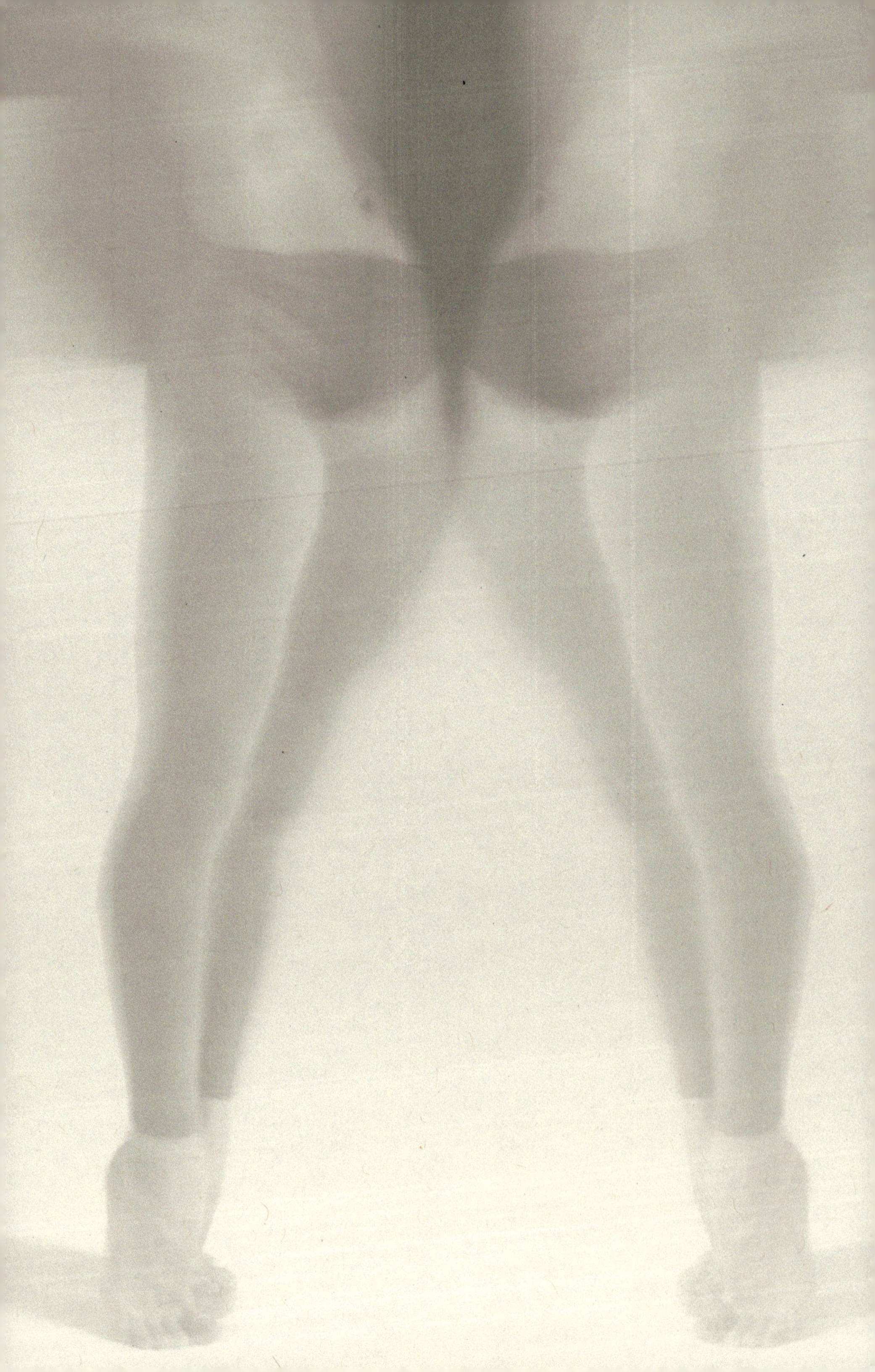

Notes and References

This book draws on research supported by the Social Sciences and Humanities Research Council.

This book draws on my life, which I have thanks to my parents, Heidi Kaplan and Jeffrey Solomon, who have given me so much more than just my life.

*

The following poems previously appeared in the following places:

“Belongings,” “Belongings III,” and “ERNEST <3 KR(~~ubin~~)YSTYNA; or, A Whole Life” in *The Malahat Review*

“Do You Know About the Flowers on the Corner of Saint-Antoine and Berri?” in *Grain*

“Dog Star” in *The Antigonish Review*

“Ernest Dances Siegfried in *Swan Lake*” in *long con magazine*

“A Failure of Science” and “A Recipe for Mug Cakes” in *The Humber Literary Review*

“(Help Me Choose a Photo of) My Engagement Ring (to Post on Instagram)” in *Touch the Donkey*

“The House on Circle Road” in *Soliloquies Anthology*

“I Try to Get My Grandfather to Tell Me Things His Parents Told Him” in *Maisonneuve*

“I’m a hole / I’m a pole / My great-grandmother was a Pole” in *The /tƐmz/ Review* and *Best Canadian Poetry 2024*

“Julia Writes to Say” in *CV2*

“Mandrillus sphinx” in *Ahoy*

“Meditations in an Emergency” and “To my colleague, Ernest, for his eyes only, in response to his confidential queries, 1934” in *Geist*

“Music” in *FreeFall*

"Nineteen, Untouched" in *& Change*

"Postmodernity Is of Course a Euphemism for Internalized Homophobia," "Analytic Frameworks," "The Seafood Buffet at Boca West Country Club, c. 1998-2010," and "Time Travel" in *Full Sentences* (Turret House Press, 2022)

Sections of "Three Sonnets About the Art in My Home" in *The Fiddlehead* and *Maybe Magazine*

"The Seven-Year Itch" in *PRISM international*

"Shopping" in *Plenitude*

"Sienna" in the League of Canadian Poets' *Poetry Pause*

"Sponsored Post; or, Grief" in *Fruit Journal*

"This isn't a gay poem." in *FLORALS* (above/ground press, 2020)

"To my dear friend Ernest at sea, 1935" in *Arc Poetry Magazine*

"To my dear friend Rubin in Bucharest, 1937" and "To Riches" in *yolk*

"Yesterday Down at the Canal" in *The New Quarterly*

"Yoo-Hoo" in *Riddle Fence* and *Best Canadian Poetry 2026*

"Overture": Thanks to Janice Rosen and Melissa Castron of the Alex Dworkin Canadian Jewish Archives for their help finding the document. Thanks to my great-aunt Cynthia Zarr (daughter of the "real" Herbert Herbert) for consenting to my accessing the document, and for the remembered "fact" about her father that is at the heart of this collection. I would not have been able to write this poem (nor would I have been able to write/complete/publish this collection) without the incredible, inimitable support and guidance of my MA thesis advisor Stephanie Bolster. I wrote "Overture" during a workshop with Liz Howard, who also provided fantastic suggestions and feedback.

"To my dear friend Rubin in Bucharest, 1937" and "Shopping" were written in response to prompts from Derek Webster, who taught the first poetry workshop I ever took. Derek's prompt to write an epistolary poem ended up being the spark for this entire collection.

"Dog Star," "Nineteen, Untouched," and "Three Sonnets About the Art in My Home" were written during sessions with my generative poetry group that includes André Babyn, Sasha Manoli, and (formerly, come back anytime) Lauren Peat.

"Reading 'Having a Coke with You' at My Best Friend's Wedding" borrows the title and some phrasing from Frank O'Hara's "Having a Coke with You." Thanks to Kayla Tanenbaum for the invitation to read the O'Hara poem at her wedding (where I read it, of course, as "Having a *Diet* Coke with You").

"Belongings": "Labor Service Will Begin Monday" is a real headline from the *New York Times* dated August 28, 1941. The ad, as described, is mostly real too.

"Yoo-Hoo" was written in response to a prompt from Lisa Richter (whose *Nautilus and Bone* (Frontenac House Press, 2020) was also supremely influential to this collection) during the Sage Hill Emerging Writers' Poetry Course.

"Sponsored Post; or, Grief," "*Mandrillus sphinx*," "To Riches," "This isn't a gay poem.," "Analytic Frameworks," "Time Travel," and "I'm a hole / I'm a pole / My great-grandmother was a Pole" were written during Sarah Burgoyne's Poetry Studios. I refer to Sarah Burgoyne as my poetry fairy godmother—she was instrumental in my getting my first chapbook published with rob mclennan's above/ground press, and has been a trusted friend and advisor, the first person to really make me believe I could take my "work," my "art" seriously (but not so seriously that I'm not using scare quotes). Thanks to Lexa Koenig for letting me use her text message for "Sponsored Post; or, Grief."

"Dos and Don'ts of Dancing for the Modern Homosexual" quotes directly (and unapologetically) from Journey's "Don't Stop Believin'." Thanks to Lauren Kendall for the memories, and to Megan Covens for the wedding where they were sparked.

"A Recipe for Mug Cakes" and "The House on Circle Road" were written as part of an occasional poetry group with Gage Michael Wheatley and Meryem Yildiz.

"Storytelling" was inspired by watching the cited YouTube video, a clip from *America's Got Talent*. Thanks to Lavender Darcangelo for her incredible talent and to Irene Cara for her iconic song.

"The Male Dancer" borrows its title from Ramsay Burt's *The Male Dancer: Bodies, Spectacle, Sexualities* (Routledge, 1995), which was a great resource and font of inspiration for this project.

"Ernest Dances Siegfried in *Swan Lake*" was inspired by Alexandra Kolb's article "Nijinsky's images of homosexuality: Three case studies" (*Journal of European Studies*, 2009).

"(Help Me Choose a Photo of) My Engagement Ring (to Post on Instagram)" was originally written for Sina Queyras's Hybrid Forms workshop. Thanks also to Sina, and to Dr. Stephen Ross, for their great and useful feedback on an earlier draft of this book, back when I was finishing up my MA thesis at Concordia.

"Julia Writes to Say": Thanks to Julia Wagner for allowing me to use her DM, and to Caroline Wagner and Eliza Cohen for their participation in the group chat.

"Yesterday Down at the Canal," "Music," and "Meditations in an Emergency" are after Frank O'Hara poems with the same titles. I wrote them as part of a creative activity with my fiancé, Guillaume Denault, in which we would both write poems (mine in English and his in French) inspired by Frank O'Hara poems, and then translate each other's work. Je t'aime, mon beau, pour tout ce que tu es. Merci pour tout ce que tu fais pour moi. Aucun des poèmes de ce livre n'existerait sans toi.

"History of the Jews in Quebec" borrows its title from Judith Weisz Woodsworth's *History of the Jews in Quebec* (University of Ottawa Press, 2021), which is a translation of Pierre Anctil's *Histoire des Juifs du Québec* (Boréal, 2017), which was an indispensable resource during the research and writing of this collection.

"The Seafood Buffet at Boca West Country Club, c. 1998-2010" was written during an inspiring workshop given by Carolyn Marie Souaid.

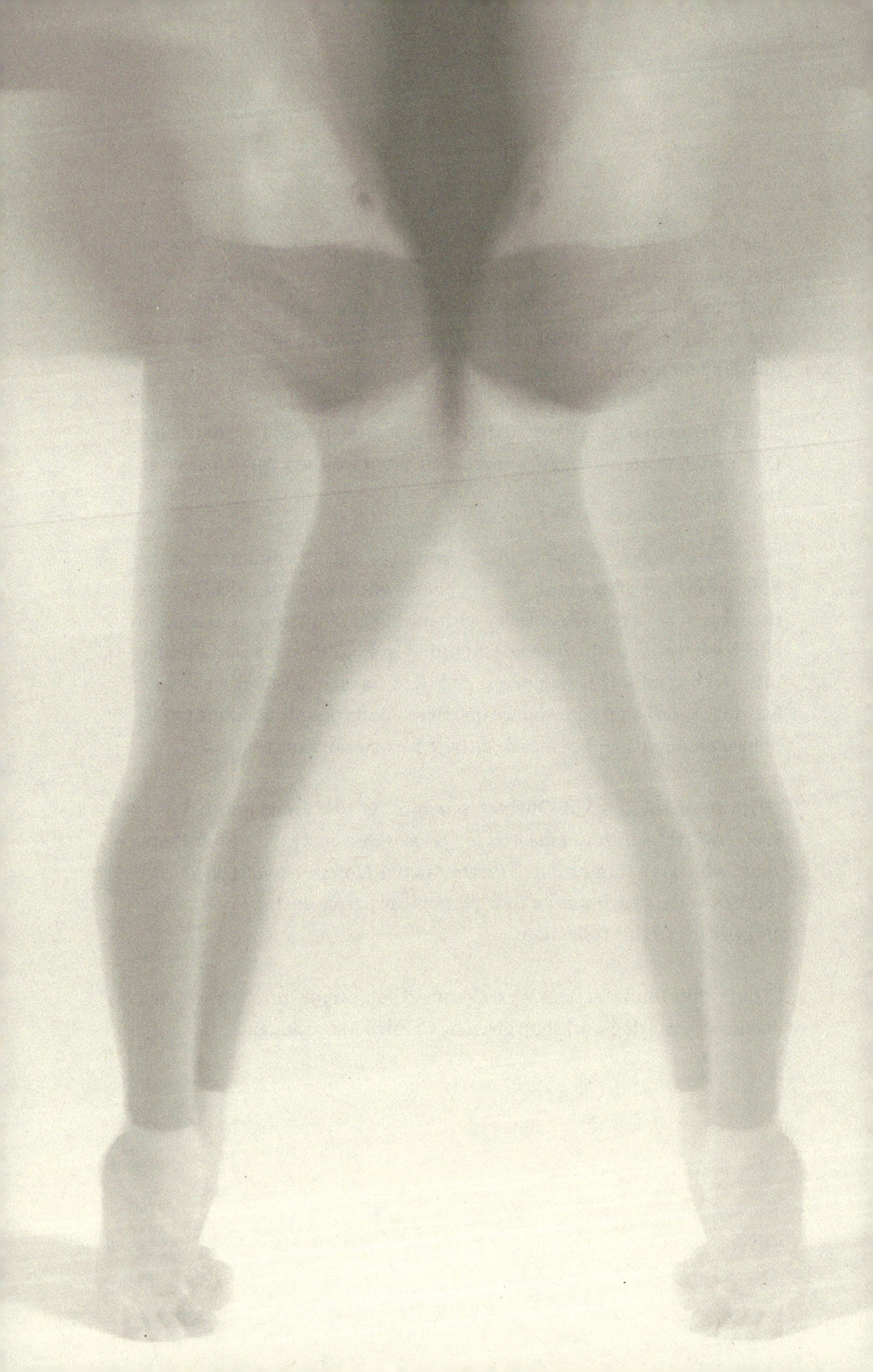

Acknowledgements

To the living—your cards are in the mail.

To the dead—I'm sorry, I thank you, and I think I love you.

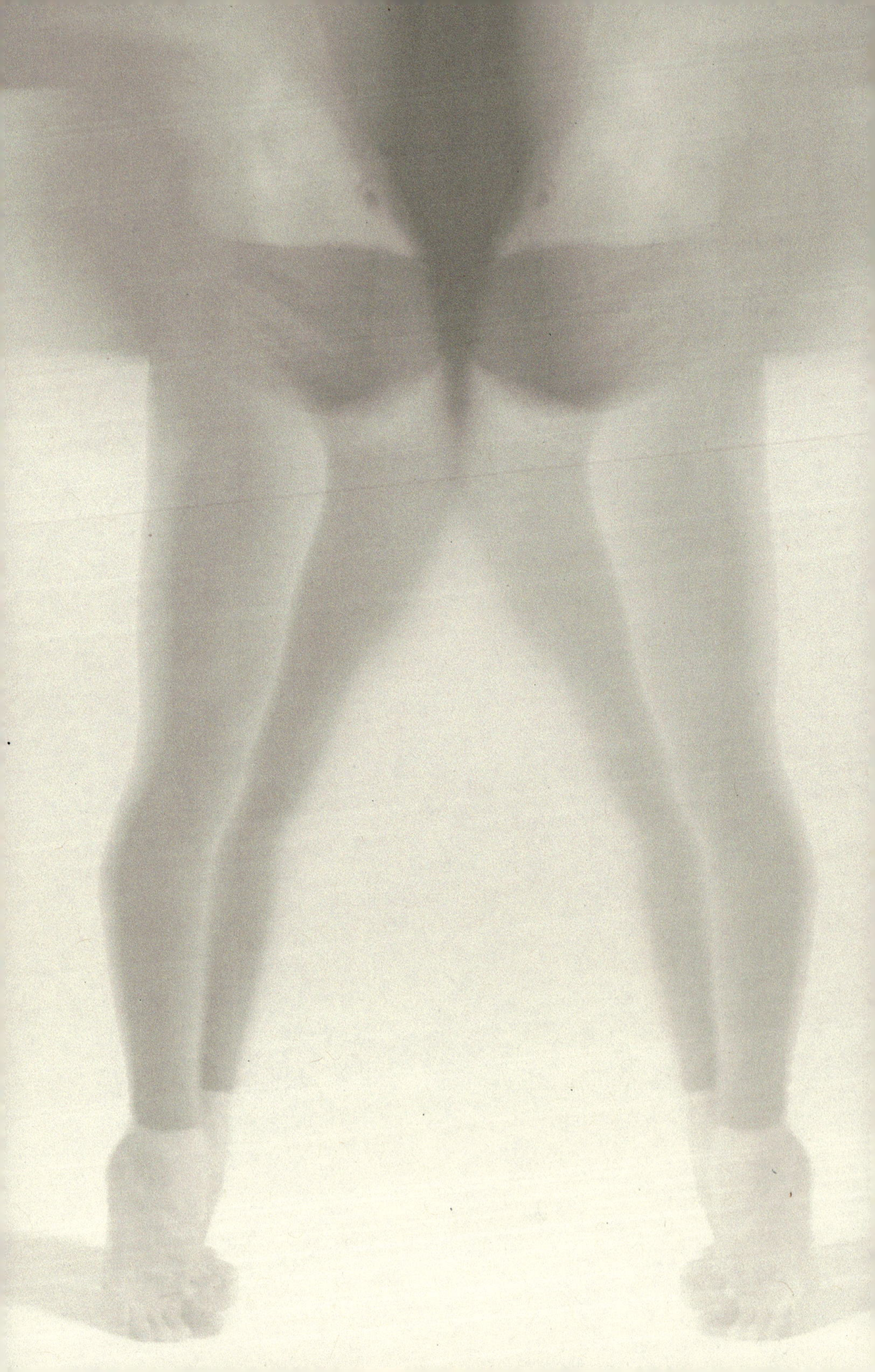

Misha Solomon is a homosexual poet in and of Tiohtià:ke/Montréal. He is the author of two chapbooks, *Full Sentences* (Turret House Press, 2022) and *FLORALS* (above/ground press, 2020), and his work has appeared in *Best Canadian Poetry, Arc, The Fiddlehead, Grain, The Malahat Review, The New Quarterly, Riddle Fence*, and *& Change*. *My Great-Grandfather Danced Ballet* (Brick Books, 2026) is his debut full-length collection.

(**Rubin's Turn**)

(I'm back I
never left I
live in the space
between your thoughts I'm
overcomplicating things I'm
just not real I
serve a purpose I'm
a symbol I'm
realer than you are

you are just one person I
am a sketch of a person I
am countless people who
did and didn't live and die

but if they lived they surely died

you, dear reader, you
are an associate god you
force me into life then you
pity my existence I
don't believe in you

I choose to live beyond these pages I
decide that I survived I
decide that I'm eternal I
say that you are dead I
say that you were never born I
say that you're a fiction I
rub my hands along my slightly sweaty skin I
tilt my head to sniff under my arms I
feel so alive when
did you last feel like this)

MIX
Paper
FSC® C100212

Printed by Imprimerie Gauvin
Gatineau, Québec